We're *All* Millennials on This Bus

*How a Return to our Pre-Industrial Roots
Can Help Us Thrive in the Information Age*

By Charles Herrick

Published by Human Fabric Publishing

Seattle, Washington

We're All Millennials on This Bus
How a Return to our Pre-Industrial Roots Can Help Us Thrive in the Information Age

© Charles Herrick 2015

Registered with the United States Copyright Office

ISBN 13: 978-1505624755
ISBN 10: 1505624754

Printed in the United States of America

Without limiting the rights under copyright reserved above, no part of this publication may be reproduced, stored in or introduced into a retrieval system, or transmitted, in any form, or by any means (electronic, mechanical, photocopying, recording, or otherwise), without the prior written permission both of the copyright owner and the above listed publisher of this book.
The scanning, uploading, and distribution of this book via the Internet or via any other means without the permission of the publisher is illegal and punishable by law. Please purchase only authorized electronic editions, and do not participate in or encourage electronic piracy of copyrighted material. Your support of the author's rights is appreciated.

Other Books by Charles Herrick

A Guide to Managing Earthlings (Business management)
IBM-style management philosophy is mixed with the author's unique style to cover everything from personnel management to corporate strategy. *What* trumps *How;* and real managers take the place of jerk bosses in this hard-hitting guide, filled with humor, war stories and personal insights. It can serve as a baseline for *Women in My Office*.

Women in My Office (Self-help and business)
Over the course of several years, the author had the privilege of being a sounding board and sotto voce advisor to women who often had no one else to talk to – including their own husbands. Whether seeking to unlock the career secrets of the male-oriented business world or dealing with infidelity, mood issues, or problems on the home front, they always got sincere counsel. Their stories are told here to help women with the many issues they face, often alone. The book has a mixture of drama and humor; kind of like life itself.

Breath of Kenya, Medicine, Mystery and Women in Rural Kenya (Non-fiction)
Alone in a primitive village in Africa to help create an economy, the appearance of a silent, deadly epidemic leads to a new, somewhat dangerous role. Charles has to play village doctor treating life-threatening diseases that most in the West have never seen. Lots of interesting insights on African life, told with humor, mixed with drama.
A greatly expanded version of the original book *Breath of Kenya*, this puts more focus on the strange rituals and taboos – especially those involving women. More little stories and some added drama.

A Checkerboard (Fiction, based on a real story)

A very white enlisted man rides through Mississippi on a bus of only black soldiers at the end of World War II. Simpson will prove the power of naiveté in changing the world around him. He settles in northern Mississippi where he courts a Southern Belle, partners with a black house painter and is taken under the wing of an aging matriarch. His cultural tutors are everywhere but led most prominently by an old black butler and a tough army Sergeant. Both support him through the cultural maze and intrigue of Southern living.

Purple Boy (Non-fiction, autobiography)

A fascinating, often light-hearted look at a pretty tough childhood, set against the backdrop of a special year running track. This in turn is woven into a psychological exploration of what is causing a sleep disorder developed in adulthood. Humor and drama bring forth the message that the human spirit can wade through anything.

Visit CharlesHerrick.com

TABLE OF CONTENTS

One	Millennials Don't Do Prefaces	1
Two	The Millennial Workplace	7
Three	Generation Me as seen by Baby Boomers	11
Sidebar	3D Communications as seen by a Boomer Writer	27
Four	Morale and the Current Fool's Errand	33
Five	Women in the Millennial Age	47
Sidebar	Women in Technology	58
Six	It's Really Hard And why you want it that way	63
Seven	Some Initial Thoughts on Getting There	69

Eight	Still Tribal after 2 Million Years	75
Nine	What Millennials Can Learn from Africa (Because All Prior Generations Did Not)	85
Ten	How Millennials Are Forcing the Inevitable	93
Sidebar	When Millennials Finally Start Voting	99
Eleven	The Humane Treatment of Earthlings (From *A Guide to Managing Earthlings*)	101
Twelve	So, Here's What You Do In Praise of the Counterintuitive	109
	Concluding thoughts A strategy for the next 1000 years	123
	Appendix Summary of Concepts A Lefthander's Guide to Management	127
	About the Author	145

Dedicated to my wife Kristy

and the many thousands of generations

of women preceding her, whose strength

and gentle nature, regardless of circumstances,

have kept our culture and our species alive

for two million years.

~~Preface~~
Chapter One
(Millennials Don't *Do* Prefaces)

This book is about changing who you are and not about changing who they are. I don't care what the topic is, this should always be the strategy in your life. It is in mine. It's what keeps you young and alive. It's what will make your company vibrant and unique in this era of the Millennial.

By reading this book, you will become a different person because you will look at your relationships with Millennials, with women, and with your fellow humans in a completely different way. How can you not be different?

When you become this new Millennial company, built around the way humans are designed, all the things that concern you about the Millennial generation will either go away or become background noise. And you will be amazed at what it's like to have employees bought in and pulling for the success of you and the organization you manage.

I'm going to reveal a critical reality in these opening pages. But it had better be quick because this book is not only designed for people who manage and work with Millennials, it is also written for Millennials themselves. And everyone knows, Millennials are about to lose focus after less than a paragraph. Which brings us to our first…

Millennial Myth: Millennials don't read.

This statement opens the way for the dialectic format you'll come to recognize in this book, because what you need is the reality (not the critical one I mentioned. It's coming).

Here's Reality:
Millennials will read just as much as everyone else but you have to *earn* their attention in each successive stage. This applies to talking and visual stuff, too.

Think of it as a game because that's totally familiar to over 95% of Millennials, who will have played over 10,000 hours of games by age 21. In a game, you get to the first level and see something you like; so you kill someone or blow something up and then you're at the next level, which in this case is the rest of the book. I promise it will go fast.

I'm hoping to end the genre of books about Millennials in which they are cast in a movie as vectors of some type of plague that can't be cured but at least needs to be mitigated. At the same time, I don't want to say that the Millennial phenomenon is just a replay of this 10,000- year old story: The older generations look down at the new arrivals and declare the end of civilization. The newbies swear they aren't going to let the same moldy mushrooms grow on their brains that turned their parents into such dull, narrow people. And then thirty years later, they are all sitting together on the front porch dissing the twenty-something hedonists and libertines that really *are* going to bring Western civilization to an end.

This time it's different. I'll tell you why. The question is: will it be good different, bad different, or just different different? The great news is we actually have a choice.

Here's another reality:
When a bunch of people, who can't possibly know for sure, all parrot the same prophecies, they are reading each other's books; so it's time look in a different direction.

Followed by this reality:
When whole generations, races, or genders get typecast, it's time to put your energy into the individuals within those groups. You'll get a wonderful return on your investment.

If you're a member of such a group, you know that your supposed attributes are neither genetic nor congenital, as much as your detractors would like to say they are. What an incredible opportunity to do a bit of self-reflection and then manage your image accordingly. You can own the place. But to some extent, when in Rome...

Both camps need to understand the thinking of the other and then make adjustments to make this work. The country is kind of depending on us all to do this.

So here's the fundamental thinking, the critical reality, that led to the writing of this book, which I will elaborate on in several of the latter chapters, especially Chapter Eight:

Myth: We have a generational issue.

Reality: Every generation has generational issues. The real problem is that we have all inherited a management system, designed for the Industrial Revolution, which violates 2 million years of genetics for how humans work with and respond to one another. In the Internet age where everyone pretty much knows what's going on, it doesn't really work anymore.

We are at a critical juncture. Either we will try to double down on old-style boss systems or we will move to humane management and thrive as a nation and as a species. I suppose there is a middle ground. We can keep trying new methods to trick people into thinking their job isn't so miserable and the managers aren't so crummy.

In the meantime, we can do some things at the generational level which will help while we're moving to one outcome or the other.

Millennials, you've got to fix some social etiquette and communication issues. The Boomers defied authority for the sake of defying authority but left most of the rules intact. You've tossed out the rules for the sake of tossing out rules and you need to go out to the dump pile and bring a whole bunch of them back.

Boomers, you've got to quit pushing Millennials to be just like you. Aren't you the guys that gave us this dysfunctional world? Do you really want Boomer redux, *in toto*?

Millennials, perk up. You do have some say in how the world turns out. It's not all baked into the cake.

Boomers, you can't change everybody and everything, so stepping on the gas pedal harder will just put your foot through the firewall of your Oldsmobile.

In the following chapters I will discuss a number of areas of the business that need to be addressed whether you have a Millennial issue or not. Thanks to pundits and professors, there are a lot of concepts floating around in the business world as accepted truths. I want to disrupt a couple of those notions and introduce some new ones. You'll see. The whole package kind of hangs together and you need all the pieces to be part of your thinking if you want to succeed.

We're ultimately going to depend a lot on the counterintuitive because that's how almost all progress is achieved. And like most things you learned that went against what seemed natural and right, whether it was gripping a tennis racket or skiing with your shoulders square to the hillside, you will soon wonder how you could have thought any other way.

We can get there. But the rest of the book will have to tell you how, because we have just reached the Millennial word and character limit.

Chapter Two
The Millennial Workplace

Read the polls. Learn some things from the polls. But don't buy everything the polls and pollsters are selling.

Millennial Myth:
The Millennial workplace is land of total discontentment.

Here's the Reality:
Work sucks. In modern times, work has always pretty much sucked because you would rather be doing something else.

One big difference now is that we have so many other things we could be doing. With transportation, communication, and entertainment so incredible and so available to just about everyone, work is now a permanent speed bump in our self-indulgent journey.

Work used to be an end in itself. The Millennials came along just after the dotcom bust and the contrast between the Roaring 1990s versus the years that followed in the new millennium was so sharp that it somehow broke the trance we were all under. Now what do we do?

As Warren Buffett once said,

> "You never know who's naked until the tide goes out."

Of course, he was talking about poorly run businesses that can hide the fact that management isn't doing the job until some hardship like a bad economy hits. But the truth is, the modern workplace was built on refinements to an ugly industrial-age social model that was only tolerable as long as everyone agreed that this is the only way it can be. Now we know that's not true. And if you don't know it, Millennials sure as heck do. We're all naked.

And it looks like the tide is going to be out for a loooonnnng time.

But what is it about work that makes it suck like a Hoover?[1]

Virtually all the polls lead to the same place. Employees don't like the way they are managed. In short, they usually can't stand their boss. Is this anything different from the way the Hebrews felt about the Egyptians when they were making bricks for Pharaoh - and every generation and occupation since? As it turns out, in terms of recent generations, what is new is the fact that it is so widespread. That shouldn't surprise you in the Information Age. Everything is spread wide pretty quickly. People in Egypt and Tunisia can look at how everyone else is living and stuff they've put up with for a thousand years won't fly anymore.

There are generational differences that we need to pay attention to. It turns out that perceptions are based partly on expectations and the contrast between the expectations of Boomers and Millennials couldn't be bigger. As a result, the

---

[1] Millennials: Hoover was a dominant brand of vacuum cleaner. It used to be synonymous with vacuums like Xerox was with photocopiers. Vacuums are those noisy machines your mom brought into your room while you were playing video games. Thank God for headphones, huh?

unhappiest people are Boomers. The polls bear this out. But despite having the biggest pouty face, they plan to stay put. They are ever the optimists, believing they can change things for the better and make the company and their bad bosses see the light. Besides, what are they going to do? Quit and move back home?

"That's a great idea!" says the Millennial. And he or she plans to do just that. He more than she, but the likelihood that a Millennial will quit when the economy gets better is about 4 times as great for Millennials as it is for Boomers. And if things don't get better, they'll quit just to change the lousy scenery. Who wants to be stuck forever at the same level in a bad video game? Your friends on the internet that you never met in person will look down on you and post weird crap on your wall on Facebook. So move to your parents basement at age 29 to preserve your dignity!

The fault for all this unhappiness in the workplace lies squarely on the shoulders of management – not Millennials. We have two things inveighing against a reasonable work environment:
- A tough cultural challenge within a bad economy
- A management layer that has gone almost an entire generation without adequate, basic management training.

People hate their bosses because their bosses are incompetent on regular management stuff, let alone being up to the task of responding to a rapidly changing world. Applying Orwellian 1984 newspeak, this is a *double-plus ungood* situation.

When I started writing this book, I asked Millennials to tell me what they disliked most about the way they were being managed. Their responses can be broken down into two general categories regarding how they feel about their version of the spikey-haired boss from Dilbert that oversees their lives every day:

- How underutilized the Millennial is compared to what he or she is capable of doing.
- How their managers simply don't have the management skills to run a meeting or plan, let alone help them with their careers, solve tough problems, coach people, motivate people, interpret the company vision for their department...

So, we have Millennials itching to apply their college degrees and their formidable technological skills, reporting to people who don't seem to appreciate those skills and wouldn't know how to apply them if they did appreciate them. And if the Millennials don't like it, there are millions more Millennials who would be willing to replace them. (82 million here or on their way to be exact!) There simply is a supply and demand situation that is not favorable to Millennials. Whenever supply is plentiful, cost goes down. Compensation is a part of the cost. It's not all that great lately, so they toss in some extra perks like beer on Fridays. But that's not what employees want most.

Employees want decent treatment and security. They want opportunity and support. These, it turns out, are a little harder to provide. It takes both commitment and competence. These come as a result of investment and training and the methodical husbandry of each crop of managers to produce exactly the right yield. Companies aren't doing that anymore.

So for the Millennial, the jobs are scarce and the jobs they do get suck. It's like the complaint convicts have about prison food:

> *It tastes terrible and they never give you enough.*

But at least it's bad for you and totally lacks nutrition!

You know what the problem is? It's those effing Millennials! They have such sh**ty attitudes, they're uninspired, they call in sick all the effing time. And they talk dirty too!

So this is what you're seeing now in the polls. You're seeing the results of a devastating mistreatment of the workforce. The polls do not offer a fair depiction of an entire generation.

It's like coming onto a battlefield after days and days of artillery fire, aerial bombardment, and nasty heavy infantry assaults and giving this report:

> *I'm not so sure about the fitness of this army. I mean, look at them. They have a bunch of wounded people, dead bodies lying here and there, great big holes in the ground everywhere, and equipment in disarray. On top of that, it's pretty clear that morale stinks.*

You have an economy in permanent malaise, management that has no professional training, a corporate attitude that puts employees third after stockholders and customers. After all that, the real Millennial phenomenon would be if you had *great* morale.

Then I *would* think they were genetically different.

Chapter Three
Generation Me As Seen by the Me Generation

This chapter will be helpful but it also has an obligatory element to it. If you don't talk smack about Millennials – at least a little bit – then you aren't being objective. You're sugarcoating.

Frankly, there's some pretty irritating things that Millennials do, so no sugarcoating will be necessary. To Boomers, some of the social habits of Millennials are so obviously untoward, offending the sensitivities of just about every culture on earth, that you wonder how they can keep doing them. If a Yanomami Indian in the Amazon rainforest knows it's not polite to be texting[2] while someone is standing there talking to you, how can a Millennial not know that? Yet Millennials often know no bounds in this regard.

Social habits change when two things occur: a change in values and a change in repercussions for violating societal norms. At just about every level, values have changed. Like all the generations that have come before, Boomers are shocked when someone doesn't treasure what they treasure and preserve traditions that they observed. And like all generations before them, Boomers have resorted to less than positive ways of addressing the issue: sarcasm, name-calling,

---

[2] There is no word for *texting* in the Xirianá language of the Yanomami. But they have several words for rude. And when they see their first Millennial texting while their son is going through his ritual for manhood, they'll probably add one more.

ostracism, gossip. All great stuff, you must admit. We humans love that stuff. Even the Bible admits that gossip is juicy:

> *The words of a gossip are like choice morsels they*
> *go down to the inmost parts.*
>
> Proverbs 18:8

So instead of sincere counseling or expressing a concern and then working through an issue, you save up all your frustration and then go share some *choice morsels* with friends and colleagues.

But the truth is, there are some big differences between generations. These show up and impact our society in a lot of different ways besides table manners or conversational etiquette. Most of these began developing long before Millennials entered into the workforce.

Before I go into a bunch of stats and start sounding academic, which this book is trying to avoid doing, let me give you an example of a situation that might explain a lot.

Imagine you're a kid playing out in front of the neighbor lady's house with a bunch of your friends. You swear and talk dirty; roughhouse, throw stuff on the neighbor's lawn, snot off to her and then leave. Later that evening, her husband shows up at your door and your mom answers. You're standing beside her. Now, if it's the 60s and your mom is from the WWII generation, she's going to hear the complaint, smack you on the back of the head and make you apologize. Later, when your dad gets home, he'll march you up the street, make you apologize again and then he'll explain how we are not that kind of a family and this will never happen again. He'll assure him of your additional punishment(s).

But what happens when we fast forward a couple of generations and your Boomer mom answers the door? Who's the bad guy now? Is it you or this intolerant, hidebound man who is trying to hurt the feelings of her precious son that is an extension of herself? You know, the boy she drives to sports practice and at least two other activities a week. You're just a kid. This man should know better than to try to push his morality on your family.

Think this is farfetched? Ask a teacher in public schools about the reaction of many parents when they hear their child has been disciplined for misbehaving. It's harsh words and then the lawyers get involved.

What did the young Millennial learn by the time the neighbor finally leaves? He learned a lot: The rules don't apply to him. Authority is not to be respected. Morality is purely situational. And there really are no consequences for bad actions. Read those four conclusions again and tell me how you could possibly have a society survive if that were really the case.

Ultimately, reality hits when that kid walks into the workplace and finds a bunch of people who think otherwise. You now have two cultures mixing with very different values and a very different belief about the consequences for violating social norms.

Perhaps the most comprehensive compilation of generational differences is found in Jean Twenge's excellent book, *Generation Me*[3]. The subtitle to her book says a lot: *Why Today's Young Americans Are More Confident, Assertive, Entitled, and More Miserable than Ever Before.* She combines data from her own research as a college professor, along with other studies, some of which have been ongoing since the 1960s involving the sentiments and beliefs of college students.

One could read no further than the table of contents to figure out the conclusions she drew. The first five read:

- You Don't Need Their Approval: The Decline Of Social Rules
- An Army of One: Me [which deals with narcissism]
- You Can Be Anything You Want to Be
- The Age of Anxiety (and Depression, and Loneliness): Generation Stressed
- Yeah Right: The Belief That There's No Point In Trying

The conclusion one draws is that never was a generation so badly set up in the history of mankind. They were told that everyone is special and that you can do or be anything you want. Then the world economy blows up, jobs and opportunities disappear, and Boomers and Xers are sitting in all the good seats.

---

[3] If there is one book we would recommend you read for a good academic discussion and background on Millennials, it would be her book.

There are many curious stats in Twenge's book, but a few will be most illustrative:

- Far more Millennials than Boomers think it's very important to become wealthy
- Far fewer Millennials than Boomers want to work hard to get rich
- The per cent of each generation who got student loans: 29% for Boomers; 64% for Millennials.
- The relative acceptance of classroom cheating (3 times as high) in Millennials vs. Boomers
- How Boomers and Millennials rate themselves on writing and math skills versus what they actually scored on the SAT. You guess which one rates themselves too high.

Perhaps the closest thing to a physiological difference between the generations is the degree to which they are hyperconnected to one another via the internet, cell phones, and social media. When we say a physiological difference, we're not exaggerating. In their book *iBrain, Surviving the Technological Alteration of the Modern Mind*, Gary Small and Gigi Vorgan make the case that Millennials are digital natives whereas Boomers and Generation Xers are to a greater or lesser extent, digital immigrants. Various new consumer technologies were introduced while Xers were growing up but virtually none were introduced to most Boomers until adulthood. As kids, we Boomers didn't have computers, microwave ovens, cell phones, cable TV, MTV, Blu-ray, or video games[4]. Portable calculators came along when I was a freshman in college and I couldn't afford one until I was a junior – and then I couldn't spring for one with memory function. CD players began replacing cassette tapes in the mid-80s. Many people thought they would not catch on because you had to buy a CD player. Besides, how much better quality could it be than a cassette tape?

What a pain! Adapt to this and then to that. Learn this. Make this thing work with that other thing. Get rid of that. No one uses those anymore. Am I keeping up? Wait. What's that? Is that…how does that work? When do the kids get home from school so they can show me how to work this thing? But to the Millennial, personal interface, digital technology was always here. Noah was probably texting on the ark and hit Mount Ararat because his GPS was lousy.

So what's the impact of having it all here from birth? You think natively. You have no digital accent. You are digital. Most Boomers have a terrible accent. That's why we mumble when we're talking tech. It is in fact the way you are wired. Your brain will wire itself if it has a specific purpose and then you will be forever changed. The reason Mozart was composing music at the age of 5 was because he began playing at the age of three. His brain was wired for music. He was music.

---

[4] Pong by Atari did not become available in homes until 1975. It was offered at Christmas time. You could only get it at Sears. Yes, that's right. Sears. That's the store that outfitted the Lewis and Clark Expedition. They sold the first Ship-Vac to Columbus. It was amazing technology to us – Pong, not the Ship-Vac.

Another great comparison is what happened when Tiger Woods was introduced to golf at the age of two. When he was 3 he shot a 46 for nine holes on a full-sized golf course. His mind and body were wired for hitting a little dimpled ball. I now have an excuse for why I can't shoot a 46 for nine holes: I'm too old. In fact, I'm way older than 3.

What I mentioned earlier about the worldwide disdain for someone who is texting while you're trying to talk to them is coming from people who are not wired the same as Millennials. At a very early age, Millennials learn to pay attention to many more sources of visual and auditory inputs at once than we ever did. Their brains are physiologically adapted to do so. We can't do this very well. They can. They lose a lot of the human nuances but they get the gist of information, music, and visual imagery while remaining totally connected.

But all this proficiency and familiarity comes at a price – sometimes a heavy price. As a Boomer, I am so thankful that there were no home computers when I was growing up. I would have loved to have a word processor instead of a typewriter and a bottle of white-out. And as I sit here and think about it, the list starts to grow. Excel would be nice. Okay, email. That would have been handy. But wait. I just crossed the line. Now I'm sitting at home developing a flat butt when I should be outside playing. What's next? Games that I play endlessly either by myself or with a bunch of other guys I'll never meet but I act like we're all part of one cool gang?

Tech is permanent. The toothpaste is out of the tube and it isn't going back in unless some Zombie apocalypse hits and we all have to sit around trying to build silicon chips by melting sand and etching circuits with a pine needle. But by having massive technology so available, we've lost something. It doesn't have to be that way but it seems we aren't working very hard to figure out what we've lost and how to get it back.

Meanwhile, we've gained some other things that aren't so good. Millennials in particular have picked up afflictions that were essentially unheard of among the twenty-somethings of the 70s. I had dozens of friends. Not a single one of them was depressed. Not a single one of them had anxiety. ADD and ADHD were not common expressions and they certainly wouldn't have been something somebody identified with or boasted about.

Boss: Fred, you did a crappy job on that report.
Fred: Oh, yeah. I have ADHD and sometimes my writing sucks.
Boss: Okay. That's good to know. Me too, sometimes.

I think such conversations have taken place on cell phones and they made it into outer space. This is good. It's what's keeping aliens from conquering us. Who would want to put up with enslaved masses, 50% of whom are proud that they're all messed up?

Alien: Fred, did you readjust that proton to protein converter?
Fred: No, man. I flaked. Totally bad day, man.
Alien: Okay, s**t. Hand me the zorba-wrench. I'll fix it myself.

This is the way Boomers often feel managing Millennials. We feel like one of us is an alien being. I'll leave it to you to guess which one. Millennials, on the other hand, feel they are being subjected to bizarre cultural demands by alien overlords. The overlords aren't in power because they have intrinsic management and leadership worth, but because they got their first and now they control the ray-gun.

You don't think so? I refer you back to Twenge's book, *Generation Me*. She has an entire chapter on the general belief held by Millennials that life is much closer to bingo or a lottery than to a strategy game. People in management were simply in the right place at the right time. Getting a college degree guarantees you little other than a mountain of student loan debt. And just look at the guys in management jobs. They can't manage because they were never trained to do so. They deal in personalities all day instead of business issues. And they are inept at the most important function of humanity in a Millennial's view: the ability to manipulate technology. Hence, they have no qualifications, so it must be luck or standing in line long enough, just breathing through your mouth, until someone taps you for a management job.

As an ex-IBM manager, serial CEO, and executive consultant, I hear this position being put forth by Millennials, I shake my head and think, "There's a fair amount of truth in what they say." Where we part ways is the notion that you can't do much about it. And that's not just because I'm a Boomer from the generation that thought we were going to change the world. It's that I came from a world where everything was determined by competition and striving. Hard work and a healthy attitude paid off.

Think of it this way, Millennials. If everyone dresses poorly, has a can't-win attitude, thinks it's not worth the effort, and you're the one Millennial who doesn't fall for that, you will win and win big. You are not the incurable cynics that much of Generation X is. You are mostly disillusioned because you were set up by social engineers in the form of teachers and government officials who told you the equality movement would work great for everyone. And now you know, being equally poor and equally powerless isn't all that great. They lied to you. And now Boomers don't understand you and don't see you jumping through a bunch of hoops like they did, so they assume you don't care.

But you do care. You care so much it's killing you. You just aren't showing it because that became uncool. Look at the depression statistics. Look at the bipolar and anxiety disorder numbers. ADD, ADHD, and Asperger's are now common diagnoses. The numbers are staggering. It went from non-existent to epidemic in two generations. Big changes are needed but are people going to make them? Are you Millennials going to be like Boomers and just step on the gas pedal harder, pursuing beliefs and habits that don't work out for you? Unfortunately, it looks like the answer is yes for most Millennials. Because what's the point, right?

Which sort of brings me to another peeve I have about Millennials: Their difficulty with the C-word: Commitment. It's worse with male Millennials than with females but even with women it's not that good. I want to be careful here, so let's get this one out of the way but get it right:

Millennial Myth:
Millennials aren't committed to anything.

Here's the Reality:
Millennials view commitment as a two-sided affair. If they don't think you're committed, then why should they be committed?

Give a Millennial something he or she believes in, show your commitment, and you'll see them at work at 2 AM making it happen. They'll commit just like anyone else. Their skepticism however, makes it conditional. That is a major generational difference. Generations that preceded the Baby Boomers kept commitments almost religiously, even if it created huge conflicts or cost them. Boomers committed and carried through, but if someone changed the deal in the slightest, they viewed that as an escape clause.

Millennials too often won't commit and too often back out on commitments, including implied commitments like showing up for work on time every single day. Whether that's true or not, it's the widely held belief of Boomers about Millennials, which means it's important for you Millennials to watch that one closely and manage your image.

One subject which tells us a lot about commitment is the age at which people get married. I know lots of Millennial women who are absolutely frustrated by non-committal Millennial men. It's like there is no sense of urgency regarding just about everything.

The results are interesting. The earnings of men and women differ if they wait until later to get married. Women tend to marry 2 years younger than men but if they wait, their lifetime earnings are higher. However, men who marry earlier in their twenties, tend to make more money eventually than men who wait until their 30s to marry. So the ideal demographic would be for women over 30 to marry guys in their early twenties. They would have to wait a couple of decades for him to grow up and quit playing video games but they would have more money to spend while they're waiting.

While tossing out the rules, Millennials are moving the country to another interesting point. According to an article by Ezra Klein in the Washington Post in March of 2013, 48 percent of all births are occurring out of wedlock. In just a few years, there will be more of what we used to call "illegitimate" babies than babies born to couples who are married. Already, the average age for childbearing is now younger than the average age for marriage.

On so many fronts, Millennials are delaying or not making the big commitments that were de rigueur in all generations past: careers, marriage, having kids, religion, political parties. The list is long. When someone doesn't commit to the more salient elements and institutions of society, they are then viewed as non-committal people. But what are they committing to? Suffice it to say, what we Boomers thought we were committing to is not viewed the same by many people in the emerging generation.

What frustrates older generations the most is the fact there is a perceived lack of decorum on all fronts: dress, manners, communication, and work habits. But whose fault is that? We saw what happened when the neighbor knocked on your door earlier. Is there someone else besides your overindulgent mother to blame? How about Bill Gates?

Bill Gates tossed out a lot of the old rules. But what did he replace them with? The answer: nothing. Microsoft has been a client of mine off and on for years and I have watched them from the beginning. Gates said software developers shouldn't have to write code in a suit. I agree. So what should they wear – anything they want? Let's try that: Jeans. Baggy jeans. Dirty, baggy, ripped jeans. Whoa! Look at that guy! His jeans are ripped from the crotch all the way down to his calf! He must be an incredible programmer because that's the only way someone could be that in-your-face slovenly! What a way to create a dress code.

Let's try communication and the fine art of management. It used to be said that there were two types of people at Microsoft: 1) People that Bill Gates yelled at or 2) People that Bill Gates was going to yell at. Is it any wonder that flame-mails, high-decibel meetings, and vicious job interviews became standard fare? I once met with the head of consulting for Microsoft. He told me about a meeting he had just attended where he had to present to Bill Gates. After making his recommendation he waited for Gates to respond. Gates, nodded his head while staring at the floor, then looked up and said, "Are you f***ing stupid or what?"

I had several interactions with IBM executives back in headquarters, including the President. I was never once asked that question. And you wonder why a company is either a solid place to work or becomes a social mess.

So we Boomers defied authority and chipped away at convention; then replaced much of it with nothing. We changed a lot of the ways of our parents, including how to rear children, and now we are shocked by what we see.

Despite all the rules that we thought didn't apply to us, here's one we boomers just couldn't find a way to escape:

As ye sew, so shall ye reap.

Sidebar on 3-D Communication from a Boomer Writer

There have been many articles written over the last few years about how texting is killing the English language. In my opinion, texting is about 90th on the list of things that are doing that. But something else is happening that I think is potentially worse and texting plays a role because it's part of the whole hyper connected world that Millennials live in. The need to be wired-in all the time says you're never fully there, where you physically are. I think it's affecting our communication and therefore, as I'll make the case, our humanness.

Having written several books, including a 200,000 word novel, I appreciate the amazing power of the English language, unique in size and depth when compared to all other languages on Earth. Goethe, the greatest of all German writers, once remarked that he would always be ranked behind Shakespeare because Shakespeare had the advantage of writing in English. But is the marvelous, living language tool we possess about to lose its magic?

In a recent small piece I wrote, I commented on a man who was dyspeptic and rude. A reviewer in his 20s told me that he looked it up on the internet and didn't get what this guy's digestion had to do with the point I was making. I told him I was using it figuratively as the opposite of eupeptic. That didn't help. Eupepsia is good digestion but a eupeptic person is also cheerful, upbeat, and optimistic. "Kind of like the Greeks and their four humors," I explained.

I took the word dyspeptic out of the final draft.

I doubt that anyone is ever going to text: "Your perpetual dyspepsia is wearing thin" when they can simply get their little thumbs going and say, "don't b such a d***head."

In previous discussions I have held, both I and my Millennial friends have come from different directions in discussing the issue of texting in the presence of others. It has centered around two different views of etiquette. A Boomer views it as almost always rude, whereas you will see two Millennials out on a date, both texting while they are having a romantic dinner. The Millennial suggestion for Boomers is, "Just say something and we'll be glad to stop." In truth, that is how they feel. I find Millennials to be incredibly honest and straightforward. They are also way more open to honest criticism than we were.

So let's put aside the Emily Post[5] aspect for a bit and talk about something that I view as having much greater moment.[6] We should consider what the impact is of being in one another's presence and not having one another's full attention. This can

---

[5] Emily Post was a woman who wrote a syndicated column for newspapers on the finer points of etiquette. She often pointed out etiquette mistakes. I think it still appears in newspapers today. It's probably going to need a new angle to attract interest with the coming generations. Maybe she should retitle her column, "Tell me! Is this effed-up, or what?"

[6] Moment is a word that is usually related to time but can also mean: *importance in influence or effect*. And I'm not taking *moment* out of the final draft.

actually include phone calls[7] but the in-person interactions are what really concern me. It is said that 80 percent of all communication is non-verbal. I have never really bought into that one. How do you even measure that? But let's agree that a lot of communication is in how we talk, not just what we say – the music versus the lyrics alone.

For illustration, let's use the song *Ramblin' Rose* by Nat King Cole. This precedes both our generations. If Rose were to receive an email or text that had this poem:

> *Ramblin' rose, ramblin' rose*
> *Why you ramble, no one knows*
> *Wild and wind-blown, that's how you've grown*
> *Who can cling to a ramblin' rose?*

It would seem like someone was saying they are done with the relationship. Yet if you hear the song, you realize it's a lament. He loves her and doesn't want her to keep wandering. He's trying to figure out how this can ever work. It's a great song, go pull it up on YouTube. Nat King Cole was the essence of cool talent.

We gesture. We pause or space our words. We smile and tilt our heads. Can all this really be replaced by ☺ or worse :) ? In the last 40 years, I have studied six other languages: German,

---

[7] People are often surprised at how quickly I end a conversation when I hear the sound of their keyboard clicking in my earpiece. This is what I hear from them: "Mmm hmmmh. Your mom's dying of throat cancer. Click click click. That's great, Charles. Click. Click. Click. Blood's coming out of her ears. Click click click. That's great, Charles. What do you mean you gotta go!?"

Latin, Arabic, Swahili, Romanian, and Spanish. Since they don't have our flexibility, all of these cultures have had to depend heavily on the non-verbal. But we in America have it all. Add to it the unique phenomenon of the American sense of humor and each communication can be a feast of concept, image, insight, emotion, information, and perception.

Millennials are weighing the value of being perpetually hyper-connected over the richness of relationship that comes with all the nuances that are engaged each time we fully interact. They're missing the joy of being human. I find the sense of humor in Millennials to be massively underdeveloped. They won't like me saying that but that brings to mind a quote from someone they will possibly never read, Frank Moore Colby, who said,

> "Men will confess to treason, murder, arson, false teeth, or a wig. How many of them will own up to a lack of humor?"

These are tough times. We need humor in all its forms from slapstick to highbrow. We'll even need some gallows humor now and again.

Another fear I have is the loss of our intuitive sense. We all have some of that. I am one of a growing number who realizes that the subject of women's intuition is more than folklore. It has a basis in physiology. The corpus callosum which divides the logical half of the brain and the emotional/creative side is much more richly supplied with nerves and blood vessels in women than it is in most men. But for either gender, it requires that the millions of mini-computers that are in our brains are invoked when we hear and see things. They process in background mode and deliver to our cognitive process a "sense" based on how all this looked under certain circumstances in the subconscious past. The more little pieces of data we store, the better. This is where the subtleties come in. This is where the tilt of the head, the smile coupled with the eye twitch, and the pursing of the lips have weight equal to a five-syllable word. We're losing this inventory and with it, we are losing some portion of the two highest levels of cognition in the entire development of humankind – humor and intuition.

Many in the Millennial clan will read what I've just said and to some extent agree – or at least acknowledge there is some truth in what I'm saying. They will then do what all young people have done for the last two million years, myself included; they'll make a note of it, try to be more aware, and at some point in the future they'll be more present when they're present. They'll draw more on that human intuitive sense. That magic.

With most advice passed on from older to younger, that works. But how do you catch up on utilizing impressions and the micro-memes[8] you never stored in the first place and

---

[8] Micro-meme. Let's go to Wikipedia on memes and then you can see why I had to invent a new word to make my point: *A meme acts as a unit for carrying cultural ideas, symbols, or practices that can be transmitted from one mind to another through writing, speech, gestures, rituals, or other imitable phenomena.* Supporters of the concept regard memes as cultural analogues to genes in that they self-replicate, mutate, and respond to selective pressures.

which can never again pass through those young, incredibly alive eyes quite the same way?

So my Boomer sensitivities have taken a different turn. I'm not sure if it's for the better or not. But where others see rudeness, I have a creeping sense of sadness and loss.

Chapter Four
Morale and the Current Fool's Errand

The Millennial issue is at its heart a morale issue. But there is more to morale than a set of symptoms.

Since I was taught that there are only two levers when it comes to morale, I did a Google search in which I entered as a search argument: *2 ways to improve morale*. Here's what I got back, in actual order of their appearance, on the first page:

- 10 Simple Ways to Improve Employee Morale – the Jostle Corporation
- Six Ways to Boost Morale that Won't Cost You a Dime – Forbes
- How to Improve Employee Morale: 14 steps (with Pictures) – Wikihow
- The Three-Stage Strategy to Improving Employee Morale – Melcrum.com
- Twelve Simple Ways to Improve Employee Morale – Technorati.com
- 10 Tips for Boosting Employee Morale – Inc.com
- How to Boost Employee Morale: 5 Tips to Make Your Team Happier – Businessbee.com
- 101 Ways to Boost Morale at Work – A PDF download from uexcel.com

I never found my list of two and it was starting to go in the wrong direction; so I quit looking. One curious thing was that all but the very last one were written by young women. Is that because they are more likely to care enough to take the assignment seriously? Or is it because the Millennial guys hadn't showed up for work yet when the assignments were passed out?

Here's the problem. A list of any length misleads you into thinking that fixing this or introducing that is going to make today's workplace fundamentally better. They are temporary fixes at best. And judging by comments I read that came with the other lists on the Internet, they stir up a lot of nasty sentiments.

So often when I meet with executives who have asked me to help them on serious problems of all kinds, I listen to their lists of 17 problems and an equal number of little solutions to address them. I wince. There are never 17 problems. There are one or two. And after hearing the many, many steps they have taken or are planning to take, I often say these words: "You are not going to fine-tune your way out of this mess."

The notion is that when you are surrounded, you can attack in any direction. But this is a bad notion. You need to find where the problem is and attack *it*. When you have succeeded and it's safe, then you can do all the great morale boosters you want. And know this: the problem that surrounds you is inevitably of your own making.

You have an identity problem and you have a culture problem. As this book is being written, the CEO of Microsoft has announced his departure. People are waiting to hear who will replace him. Whoever it is will have to address both these issues: What is Microsoft? And how are we going to treat one another going forward? A lot of people want them to find the next Steve Jobs. That sounds great. But unless the new Steve Jobs of Microsoft addresses identity and culture, great ideas will languish or be ripped to shreds. The new CEO has to introduce new ideas that will signal what the new identity of the company is going to be and he or she has to do it while simultaneously changing the way Microsofties treat each other from the top to the bottom of the hierarchy.

So let's start with a myth:
To fix morale, you take unhappy people and do fun things that make them happy.

But here's the real rule:
To fix morale you must change the company and become completely different people.

That sounds way more simple than doing 14 things – or 101. However, there is a big difference between simple and easy.

The two morale levers are these:
1. Make people feel that the company is going to succeed.
2. Perform on a <u>daily</u> basis, the three utility functions of management:
   - Communication
   - Delegation
   - Recognition of performance

Let's use my experience at BEST Consulting as an example of how to do this. You will see that you have to change everything.

BEST was a staffing company that supplied other companies with developers, data base people, project managers, tech writers, and many more IT specialists. They usually did this one or two people at a time, with just a few small projects of their own here and there, where they owned the full responsibility of developing a product or new function for a given client.

Morale was horrible among the 700 employees, spread over several offices in the western US. Turnover was 55%. We were in the middle of the dotcom boom, yet our growth over the last 3 years had gone from 15% to 6% to 0%. We were profitable, doing $6M in net income on $60M in revenue. But very little of that money was reinvested back into the employees. Not much, that I could see, was going back to the community.

I had my hands full. I started with the Seattle office which had 278 employees. Here I worked with the five former owners, some of whom thought I was a snotty ex-IBMer who didn't fully understand or appreciate their business. I had negotiated as part of the agreement to hire me that I could change the business model to offer more of the heavy project work that IBM was known for. They were suspicious and unsupportive – sometimes undermining me and allowing people who reported to me to go around me to them.[9]

---

[9] Never panic when this happens. Just work your plan and don't allow decisions to be made by anyone that are within your purview. This includes your boss.

I knew there were two things that were key: changing the business model, which would change our identity and fixing the high turnover rate which would require us to change the way we treated one another at every level.

Here's a good place to talk about a greatly misunderstood subject: vision.

I was recently the guest speaker at an informal roundtable of Seattle-area executives. It included CEOs and a number of high ranking executives from companies headquartered in Seattle that are household names. I was asked to talk about my perspective on the Millennial "problem." Before I could launch into my annoyingly upbeat discussion, a couple of comments were made that were perfect for me to introduce the philosophy that underlies much of what I preach.

The first statement was made by an executive who said to another exec supportively, "Yeah, I agree with Jack Welch: you should constantly be getting rid of your bottom 10% of employees." To this I asked, "What if there is no bottom?" There's more to come on this one.

The second statement was when I was asked about offering a vision statement. To this I responded, "What's your definition of a vision statement?" His answer was pretty standard. "It's a compelling portrayal for the employees of what the company will be doing three to five years down the road. It answers the question, 'Where are we headed' and it gives people a common purpose." The others seemed to agree. And I would have agreed had I not experienced otherwise.

I told him that to me it had to be much more dramatic than that. It has to tell people what you collectively are going to become. And whatever that is, to be effective and motivating, you must become a different entity than who or what you are now. Because once you know who you are, you will know what to do. And if you can outline who you are becoming, then you are already that entity today.

He asked me how that fit with the common example used where John F. Kennedy stepped to the microphone and said about the space race with the Soviets: "First, I believe that this nation should commit itself to achieving the goal, before this decade is out, of landing a man on the Moon and returning him safely to the Earth."

That is a great vision statement. It's very clear and compelling. But it's not a vision. Go read the whole thing and you'll see that he really laid out a plan so that everyone would believe it. Because once we believed it, we became different people. We were the guys who were going to the moon! We were no longer in a me-too, tit-for-tat. They launch Sputnik. We launch a satellite. They circle the earth 3 times with Yuri Gregarin. We send Alan Shepherd up and bring him right back down. What are you then? Just a bunch of guys doing space stuff. No wonder morale at NASA sucked.

Suddenly, we were the guys who just declared we were going to the moon. We dreamed big, put it out there, and we did it. We had to do a million things to make it possible like somehow build the biggest rocket ever, condense computerization, build a lunar lander that could launch itself again, invent tang and dustbusters. That's what you do when you dream big. You change everything.

So let's return to earth and my dull little problem. I said we were no longer going to be a business where we just did staffing. We were now going to compete with IBM, Ernst and Young, Anderson, and the other members of the Big 5. We could do that because that's what I knew how to do, I declared it, picked two industries to target specifically (Telecom and software companies) and then hired more people like me who could pull it off. At the same time, I was going to hang onto the staffing business so I could have access to all the companies I wanted and I could avoid the big revenue swings associated with firing up large projects and then having them come to an end. People believed me. We were on our way to becoming the dominant IT consulting player in the Northwest. That's who we were.

At the same time, I went after turnover. It was composed of two things: people quitting and people being fired or laid off. Often, the firings were arbitrary. There was zero loyalty or commitment in either direction between employees and management. I fixed that. I made it absolutely miserable to fire anyone. In fact, you couldn't fire anyone without calling me first and explaining why you were going to do something so awful to another human being. The first two branch managers that tried it took it a bit too casually. They couldn't answer my questions very well:
- When did the employee first show signs of not cutting it?
- What did you tell him?

- Did you put him on an improvement plan with clear milestones to be achieved?
- Did you seriously work with him to help him turn around his performance?
- Did you document anything?

So now you're going to send a guy home at 2 in the afternoon to tell his wife they no longer have an income – that they can forget the big vacation, putting their kid into that good college. She can forget about security for a while and she can start scrimping and tightening up and keeping a bold face for the kids. I let them know that I had a much bigger problem with someone who was willing to do something so gruesome as to cut off a family's income than I had with an employee who was underperforming. And to do it with such a casual attitude was infuriating.

That word spread.

And then a wonderful thing happened. I came back from lunch and found out that the personnel VP, part of the old guard, had fired two guys while I was at lunch. His reasoning was that the project manager had brought these guys in to him, told him about how they had gotten really sideways with the client, and we couldn't let them go back to the job. So he fired them. I asked if they had committed an act of violence. Nope. Stole something big? Grabbed some woman in the copier room? Nope. Nope.

I thanked him and ended the meeting. I then had my secretary call the two guys that got fired and I brought them back to work. They hadn't been read their Miranda rights.

That word spread. Firings dried up. All of a sudden, managers were doing two things: Getting people's skills up and hiring people far more carefully because they just might have to keep 'em. They also documented their work like professionals.

Next, I looked into what was causing all the turnover. There were a lot of reasons:
- No loyalty
- Nothing special about our company
- Lots of other places to work
- We had a habit of converting someone to hourly (not paying them) once they came off of an assignment, so why not quit when you see your project coming to an end and find a job while you're still getting paid?
- If you were stuck on a long project and a new version of the software in which you specialized got announced, then you were going to become back-level real quick. So go someplace where you can be involved with the new version, learn it, and keep your skills up so you can maintain your value in the marketplace.
- People wanted a career path that would allow them to advance into management but no one ever had such discussions with them.
- People wanted to earn more money throughout the company including sales, administration, project management and development.
- They weren't treated with respect. No one ever said, "Thanks" or "Good job!"
- Once on assignment, no one ever talked to them.

The first two were easy to address. We made our company very special and we began treating people like they were special. The vision sold and loyalty flowed with it. Then we built, staffed, and ran our own internal education company to train people and keep their skills up. To pay for it, we opened it up for a fee to clients. We made $2 million the first year. Now you could be on a project and take free after-hours classes to keep your skills up.

We created a "bench" for people coming off of an assignment. The previous owners had only allowed a bench of three people at a time. Everyone else had been put on hourly "pay." We now allowed the bench to expand as needed. I had already increased the number of salespeople and taken away a lot of non-sales work from them, so they had a lot more time to find homes for the people on the bench. But that wasn't good enough. We created three virtual benches for:

- People *about to* come off assignment
- People who had expressed a desire to have new skill-building experiences.
- People who were unhappy with where they were

I put a superbly gifted bench manager in charge of the whole process which often involved as many as 80 people. It became a business unit of its own.

Turnover plummeted. I had announced a target of taking it from the industry standard 55% down to 25%. No one believed me. They were right. We hit 17% the first year and 12% the second. Almost no one quit anymore.

In the meantime, I instituted my own short-version of IBM management school, personally training in groups of 15, every single manager in the company and then every new batch that came in thereafter as we grew. The managers learned to focus on *what* instead of *how*. They learned to focus on business issues and not deal in personalities. They learned and then practiced in role play how to deal with tough personnel situations. They learned how to run a productive meeting, coach, counsel, and critique people. They learned that if you de-personalize the management process, you can have much better employee relations.

They learned how to perform the three utility functions of management: communication, delegation, and recognition of performance. I then followed up with ways to measure this. I also demonstrated it via MBWA (management by walking around). We created and then lived a new management culture.

We also took an interest in the community. We announced that the Seattle office was "adopting" the Union Gospel Mission. We had a dinner for 500 employees and their spouses one evening just after Thanksgiving in which both I and the executive director of the Union Gospel Mission, Herb Pfiffner, presented the story of this remarkable organization that started out by helping street people back in the 1930s and now had a family support center and a shelter for battered women. The employees were all over it. We set up a giving tree that had requests from the people in the mission. We filled boxes and boxes with donations. The day after the announcement, a couple of employees came into the office and wrote checks for

$1000. Teams of employees self-organized to go down to the various mission sites to paint and clean. It was tearfully wonderful.

To deal with all that we were asking of people, we instituted variable pay for just about everyone in the company including admin because it's really helpful when you are trying to change behavior to pay extra for the new behavior and the results that come with it. Variable pay is critical to companies who wish to grow. But you have to be simple and specific. You can't just throw everyone into a pool and pay them all extra if you hit it. That can be a secondary target but not a primary coefficient of variable pay. You have to do it right. We got it right.

As a result, we went from 0% growth to 74%. In two years we went from $60M in revenue to $130M and almost tripled our profits. Morale was sky high.

We changed who we were and then we knew what to do. We changed everything. That's what you do.

We pulled the two levers:
- Everyone believed we were going to succeed.
- Management practiced the three utility functions of management on a daily basis.

We didn't need crazy perks. We didn't need birthday cakes. We just did our jobs and took care of our people. We provided both security and meaning.

I cherished my employees. I protected them. I loved my job. I viewed myself as a servant. I was two-fisted and gregarious and probably not as meek and mild as I should have been. I'll admit I had a few detractors and some out and out enemies. But I still saw the role of management as one of service to make it possible for the people out on the front lines to do their jobs. And they needed to do it in peace and security, not looking over their shoulder to see if they're in the bottom 10%.

Maybe there's one more lever: Care so much about your people that they can see it in everything you do.

Chapter Five
Women in the Millennial Age
(Which includes the last 2 million years)

First, I'll tell you the three magic rules to keep in mind regarding women in the workplace that have been true since shortly after we were expelled from the Garden of Eden. Then, I'll tell you what has gotten in the way of observing those very simple rules because despite a lot of progress since women were allowed to vote, smoke, and drive,[10] we still have a ways to go. And now that the social engineering is being led by legislators, suit-happy lawyers, people with a big chip and their shoulder, and the PC police, it looks like we might be playing out Zeno's paradox[11] – not for mathematical reasons but because they keep moving the wall!

So, let's start with the three rules. These were derived by the following scientific process: I asked a bunch of women some fairly general questions about the workplace. I was actually doing so for another activity I'm engaged in regarding putting

---

[10] Except in Saudi Arabia where they can do none of these things. I'm really struggling with the ban on women driving in a country where they are essentially servants. You would think it would be handy to have them run down to 7-11 and pick you up a pack of smokes. I wonder if it's the same logic as what kept English women riding sidesaddle for so many years. I could design a car around that one, if someone will please clarify.

[11] Zeno was a Greek mathematician who pondered: If you cross a room and with each step you halve the distance to the opposite wall, can you ever reach the opposite wall? Since space is infinitely divisible, the old answer was that you can't reach the wall. Then Newton came along with calculus and the theory of limits, proving that you will in fact reach the wall. But you knew that.

together an organization that will fund women's health initiatives worldwide. From those questions, I perceived some recurring themes which I summarized into three rules. I asked those women and several others if the rules were correct. The general response was, "That's about right." Science was served.

How is this scientific? That's easy. When you ask women a reasonably serious question, close to 100% of them will give you a thoughtful answer; unlike men – especially younger men – 50% of whom will give you a wise-ass answer; 50% will give you an answer that they think will make them sound smart, and 30% will give you a very thoughtful answer to your question. I know that adds up to more than 100% but that's just another reason why conducting such exercises with women is way more scientific.

So here are the three rules you should know about women in the workplace:
1. Women are highly social, more so than men, and they want to feel they are a part of the social fabric, not a cog in an organic machine.
2. Women want their work to be meaningful and their contributions recognized, even if it's just the merest acknowledgement. (By the way, husbands, this applies on the home front, too).
3. Women would like to do their work without being bugged by irritating guys. (Ditto on the home front).

There you go. Now is that so hard? Do you think you could design an HR policy around that very short list? Before you try, let's discuss some things that I never hear anyone talk about because they imply that there might possibly be actual differences between men and women. And we all know that can't be true because our journalism professors have done extensive research and no further discussion or research is needed or permitted.

Let's look at the first point because it is the most critical element in forming the glass ceiling. It's tempting to say that it boils down to the Golden Rule: Treat others the way you want to be treated. But it doesn't – not when there are gender issues involved. Men treat one another and are willing to be treated in ways that are highly offensive and annoying to women. When was the last time you saw a woman pull a spontaneous practical joke on someone? How often do you hear women sitting around making crude noises and laughing? When was the last time you saw a group of women off by themselves having a contest on an endless list of meaningless objectives, such as who can toss a pencil behind his back and make it stick in the ceiling tiles?

As a high school student I worked in an old furniture warehouse that had spiders. Some of them were very large. At various times a couple of guys would each decide he had found the biggest spiders ever. Then they would put the two spiders into a Styrofoam cup and try to get them to fight to the death. Despite numerous creative attempts to incite arachnid mayhem, the spiders pretty much ignored each other and tried to find ways to crawl out of the cup. This happened about a dozen times, which is exactly twelve times more than it has happened in any group of women, anywhere on the planet.

So what's my point? As it regards the first rule, it has to do with cooperation, which is core to forming a society and being social. Men will cooperate where there is a common purpose but then they will compete on everything else. Whereas women tend to be broadly cooperative and don't view stuffing the other guy as a desirable pursuit.

This affects women in two ways because men tend either to take advantage of a woman's cooperativeness or they misunderstand it and confuse intra-group cooperation with an inability to compete on the battlefields of business with the company's real competitors.

In my career conversations with aspiring employees and even executives, the philosophical differences between men and women were stark. Women believe you should move up the ladder based on merit. Men believe they naturally deserve to move up the ladder and now it's just a matter of proving they have met some undefined minimum standard and that they are more deserving than the other guy to move forward.

I once heard the founder of the national organization 85 Broads talking on the radio. She was a Wall Street executive. She made the comment that in all her time in management, not a single woman had ever come to her and asked for a promotion. Is it possible her experience is just an anomaly? I have had thousands of employees and lots of them have asked me for a promotion. Only one or two of them was a woman. Most promotions involving women have been entirely at my instigation. Many of those women felt it necessary that I know all the facts as they pointed out possible reasons why they weren't qualified or they might not do very well in the job I was *pushing* them into.

Is this lousy self-esteem? Possibly. But I think there is something else at play here. Women want the organization as a whole to succeed. They feel the best qualified people should be running it. They also feel that all facts should be known in making that decision. They do not want to be responsible for running an operating unit if they aren't the best fit. That rarely stops a guy from taking a job he can't really handle. He'll try to fake it and hope the Peter Principle doesn't catch up with him before he fakes his way into the next job. Have you ever worked for a completely incompetent idiot? This is where they come from. And then they adopt all kinds of reprehensible and repressive behaviors to maintain control since natural leadership is out of the question with a group of people who simply don't respect them.

The issue of the glass ceiling for women is a serious one. In my opinion, it is hurting American business and needs to be addressed by an insightful, thoughtful, and aggressive affirmative action program.[12] This must come from the top. Otherwise, middle managers and executives will tend to bring forward candidates that fit the conventional model: steely-eyed, assertive, goal-oriented, tough, and so forth. All of these are relative and therefore all of them are measured on some ill-

---

[12] At the corporate level, not the governmental level. We really don't want legislators running our businesses. Have you seen how they run the government, a place where they work every day? To become a career legislator requires a curbing of the instinct followed by the rest of the animal kingdom in which one does not soil one's own nest.

defined scale, with *managerialness* or *execuitveness*, like beauty, clearly in the eye of the beholder. The eye of the beholder will always be adjusted to the eye of beholder they report to, unless counterintuitive principles are applied.

There are two myths to deal with here.
Myth 1: A person who is hesitant to claw past his or her peers, must be unable to tough it out with the company's competitors.

Myth 2: If you're unwilling to inflict pain on others, you must be thin-skinned yourself and therefore not tough enough to be the boss.

The counterintuitive principle at play here is that <u>leadership is a "draw" skill, not a "push" skill.</u> You *draw* people to you by your competence and your understanding of what needs to be accomplished and then you work with your people to see that the right things are getting done by the right people. This is only counterintuitive because between stereotype-driven television shows and the unfortunate numbers of pushy people who *do* get ahead, we think that pushy bosses are somehow okay and possibly more effective. I've written a whole book explaining otherwise;[13] so I won't go into it here, but a woman's tendency to be cooperative, merit-driven, and non-pushy is working against her. Selection against those traits is working against the company.

---

[13] *A Guide to Managing Earthlings*

Let's look at item #2, the desire for meaningful work. If that seems like it applies to everyone on earth, then what's the big deal? And what's that got to do with women? It's because we men often ignore that rule when it comes to women. They're such good sports.

One way to get into trouble with the leading scientists of our culture (media pundits who learned from a journalism professor with a pony tail) is to say that men and women are different in any way other than some obvious curves and other physical features.[14] So, if I'm going to go up against the science of pony-tailed journalism, I had better come equipped with my own science. And here it is:

Women appear to have a good sport gene.

Here's the logic: There are a ton of tedious or otherwise undesirable jobs that men just won't do but women will. Therefore, women must be more suited to them and women should do them. Besides, they don't get angry or wait for you in the parking lot with a broken beer bottle after work, so they must not mind.

Even though a lot of the old-style, stereotypic "woman" jobs have disappeared from the modern corporation – file clerk, keypunch operator, switchboard operator – the tendency to

---

[14] Even this is being worked over by the frustrated cultural advance guard. Have you seen movies lately where lightweight women stand toe-to-toe with a burly guy and knock him down with a roundhouse punch? That doesn't happen on this planet. I used to box. It's hard to hit someone effectively, even if you're a strong guy. It takes practice as well as strength. Where do wispy women go to practice butt-kicking?

give women on the team the tasks that are a bit drearier is matched only by the tendency for women to take on such tasks. Women don't like these tasks any more than men but their cooperative spirit in sharing the load is compounded by men's competition for the better assignments. The primary solution to this problem for most companies is good, sensitive, involved management.

The best solution however, is culture. You simply live a certain way that everyone knows is right. When it comes to women, it will take a little extra effort because we need to get past the last 10,000 years of human culture which has treated women as little better than property.[15]

I believe that the proper treatment of women and the subsequent progress that will result from seeing women free to achieve excellence on their own terms is the single most important measure of real progress. It is also an area, done right, that will see a surprising consensus between liberals and conservatives, Republicans and Democrats, feminists and traditionalists. The latter convocation is key.

When someone claims to be a traditionalist on gender issues, it seems they need to constantly redefine themselves because what was acceptable forty years ago is laughably out of vogue today. It's a dark suit and black oxfords with white socks. But what if we could quickly come to terms with this issue such that in forty years we won't be laughing once again at those troglodytes back in 2015?

---

[15] That is the fundamental issue which a group of us are forming an organization to address on a worldwide basis.

In my time in management I have observed a number of differences, in general between men and women. Unfortunately, I never learned to manage people in general. I always managed each person as an individual. That being said, one of the *general* differences between men and women is that women tend to care more about the process and men tend to be just a little more concerned about the results. Process-oriented vs. results-oriented would appear to favor men, if you note that my theme for managers and execs is to focus on *what* instead of *how*. It also raises the question: are men a naturally better fit for management than women?

First, you will note I'm talking about process-<u>oriented</u> vs. results-<u>oriented</u>. Orientations can be modified. Since focusing on *what* implies that being results-oriented is more naturally aligned, does this mean that the only ones who need to go to my reorientation camps are women? The answer is no. When I say *how*, I am talking about the course of action to get there. You want this to be an individual thing. Women often get there by a different course of action than men, if allowed to do so. But there is also the question of mode, mood, and scenery, which is something that overly results-oriented <u>bosses</u> quite often ignore, causing suffering by their employees. I care a lot about that part of process and I take action against managers that report to me who ignore it.

Following the rules, which women do better than men, sounds admirable but it can be taken too far. During World War II, when individual American units faced individual German units, the Americans tended to win, not because of superior fighting ability but because of greater ability and willingness to modify the orders of their superiors. Women need to do this more often. Managers and executives need to encourage this and, what is more important, they need to be willing to overlook the fact that the rule book was tossed out even when the results are less than expected. Look at what they were trying to accomplish, discuss it collegially, agree on modifications for the future, and move on.

Generally speaking, I work on men to be a little more focused on making the journey enjoyable and I work on women to be willing to put down the rule book and take acceptable risks. Women adapt. Their employees appreciate it and so do I.

You know, you don't have to wait for society to change to effect this yourself. You can do it today. If you're a manager, you can start your own program and you don't even have to announce it.

It starts with observing. It starts with noticing how terrific women are. They are special and in many ways, they are different, despite modern social engineers stating otherwise and declaring such sentiments as patronizing. Humans have known this for 2 million years. But, like our modern diet and our modern management practices, we stick by our newfound societal concepts, overturning millennia of wisdom at our peril.

There is only one way you can truly appreciate women in the workplace and that's to let them do their job their way. This is the essence of my what-versus-how management philosophy outlined in *A Guide to Managing Earthlings*. It works for everyone but we seem to let it slide a bit when it comes to women not measuring up to male behavioral standards, as if that were a meaningful business measurement in itself.

If you can establish a collegial relationship, agree on what needs to get done, and then assist when asked for help, you will in time be impressed. It may also explain why, over time, I often tend to end up with slightly more women than men in the management of organizations I run. Ultimately, management is a profession. I'm just looking for people to get the job done. By not looking at *how* people do their jobs, I am freed up to do my job as the Chief What Officer.

In the meantime, my message to men is that you quit taking advantage of the good sport gene that women seem to carry on the X chromosomes. And don't let others do it, either. That means you have to be vigilant and watch for it because women usually won't complain or pursue iconoclastic measures.

Don't confuse cooperation with the inability to compete. Don't confuse complacency with true acceptance. Question patterns of the past, because they were wrong on so many fronts.

When you get to the point where you can survey your actions versus your policies, see if you followed the 3 Rules for Women that I stated at the beginning of this chapter:

1. Proactively honor their desire to be part of a social fabric
2. Give them meaningful work and acknowledge contributions
3. Don't bug 'em. Don't let irritating guys bug 'em.

SIDEBAR
Women in Technology

Here in the Seattle area, in what is known nationally as a socially liberal state, there is pressure to conform to an egalitarian world that is blind to gender, race, age, and so forth. The pressure comes from all directions but often it comes from the legislature, news media, and lawyers. Based on what I'm hearing, the results are mixed. You have very progressive companies like Starbucks who are on it all day every day. But then you have the high tech firms.

For the last few years, news and feature articles have been coming forth on a fairly regular basis pointing out that for all the talk and good intentions, the tech world is still a guy's club. A recent article by Geekwire's Jeff Reifman on Amazon, a company heavily dependent on a technology infrastructure, slammed the organization for, among other things, its lack of workforce diversity:

> *Last month, Amazon released its diversity numbers. While the company reports 63% of its worldwide workforce is male, it's likely closer to 75% male in the company's Seattle technology headquarters; that's the company's overall managerial ratio and close to Microsoft's technical ratio. The Rainbow PUSH coalition called Amazon's report "...intentionally deceptive, as the company did not include the race or gender breakout of their technical work force."*

Jeff, let me tell you what it's like running a tech company in Seattle, because I've done it. The overwhelming majority of your applicants are males. The majority of those males are white, followed by Asians. When you're building a tech firm or a company with a strong technology infrastructure like Amazon, the overwhelming majority of the people available and qualified to do the job are men.

Tech development is not like other jobs where there is an entry level and the company spends a bunch of time letting you work with senior people to learn the job. Guys come right out of high school or college knowing how to do some amount of software development or systems work. They get whatever job they can that will allow them to apply their skills and then they get better and better (by doing) until they have level 5 skills. Colleges are teaching software development and other computer science/computer engineering courses. Go walk into one of those classrooms at the University of Washington toward the end of the series where you finally have some commercially applicable skills and tell me how many women you see.

As I say, it's not like sales or administration where you can be a low-paid trainee for a while in hopes that you will at some point be productive. You can't sort of write code. The computer won't get it. It either works or it doesn't.

Now that you have your building full of white and Asian males constructing your whole company infrastructure for you, who are you going to promote into management? I would like to see Jeff Reifman start a fast growing tech firm and try to build it with a rainbow team and only 30% white males. Your first several million dollars had better go into building the most powerful recruiting team on the planet, because level 5 developers who know several coding languages and have three or more years' experience in Agile software design methodology and who also happen to be black females are going to take some really solid searching techniques. And a whole lot of money.

Eventually development languages will become higher level and driven by the machines. While that's happening, new types of technology are going to emerge. And unless there is a major push to get girls into a STEM mindset, starting in elementary school, with real results by the time they graduate from high school, the tech landscape is going to continue to be male dominant. But the STEM initiatives for girls must actually produce the real result of getting girls interested in these areas of education. They can't just pass through the program. They've got to pop out of those classes with a real desire to pursue engineering or computer science. If they do, the doors will be open.

Here's the dilemma we face as a nation that prides itself on fairness:
- If you try to force tech firms to hire based on anything other than capability, then they will be at a clear disadvantage in a global battle that is getting increasingly nasty.
- If you just keep building your workforce with white and Asian males, you will perpetuate a cultural norm that discourages women and minorities.

Such an intensely difficult problem has only one solution in America: sue somebody.

I raise this issue and state these facts, not in an attempt to honor and perpetuate the status quo, but because I believe it is so important that we don't have a nation full of people thinking they will never get a shot at the good life because people are actively plotting against their gender, race, weight, or any other attribute. Nor do I think it's okay to push the notion that while people may not be actively discriminating against women in the tech world, they are somehow either oblivious to or okay with the fact that every time women get on the tech bus, they somehow end up in the far back seats. They're not okay with it. They're not un-okay. To most people, it is what it is.

There is now proof that left handed people make 6% less than right handed people. I'm furious. As a left handed person, not only are tools and everything else made for right handers, now I get paid... Wait. I make a lot of money. Always have.[16] But I'm still going to tell every left handed kid I meet that he has no chance of getting a fair shake. How does that sound?

Better yet, I'm going to go on television as a self-proclaimed spokesman for lefties, sit there with a long face, and be interviewed by an unctuously sympathetic talk show host about how hard it is. I'll be inconsolable. And I'll be one more

---

[16] If you don't count working as: a gas station attendant, janitor, waiter, cook, warehouse worker, dialysis technician, lawn mower...

messed-up[17] victim in this once great nation of people who are now divided on every characteristic.

Jeff and others are exhibiting the knee jerk response that is tearing up America. When we see one group over or under-represented in any measurement, we assume foul play and we want [government] action to correct, even if we can't actually recommend any specifics ourselves.[18] Understanding is out of the question unless it is an effort to accumulate facts that will support the theme of victimhood.

Fortunately, the whole world isn't one big tech firm. But to the extent that tech comprises a certain portion of a given company's workforce, the percent of the employee base that is white male and Asian male will be skewed concomitantly.

Regardless of the mix, you will still have a company full of individuals who want to be treated fairly in the Millennial age. That's what this book is trying to address. It's a real opportunity to do it right, for the first time, since most of the old rules have lost the efficacy to dictate our every action.

---

[17] The word messed-up is a replacement word. Figure it out.
[18] Just out of curiosity, I called a couple of big guitar stores. It turns out that about 90% of their customers are guys. What should we as a nation do to get more girls forming rock bands? You keep reading. I'm calling the Pony-Tailed Professor Hotline.
Is it possible that men and women have different..............naaaahhh.

Chapter Six
It's Really Hard
(And why you want it that way)

It's supposed to be hard.

There is a pivotal scene in the movie *A League of Their Own*, starring Tom Hanks, who plays the part of a washed-up major league baseball manager, now managing a woman's professional baseball team. It was set during the period in World War II when men's baseball had been suspended so the men could join the war effort.

Tom Hanks' character was pretty hard on the women; treating them the harsh way old-style coaches typically treat male athletes – berating them in public, picking on them for crying, and humiliating them for any mistake. You know, sports stuff.

This didn't sit well with his star athlete, played by Gina Davis. As they were loading the bus to head for the next game, Hanks sees her dressed in civilian clothes, carrying a suitcase to a car in the driveway. He approaches, tells her she will regret it all her life because "Baseball is what gets inside you. It lights you up! You can't deny that." She responds in staccato, "It just got too hard."

Hanks then leans forward and explains to her, "It's supposed to be hard. If it wasn't hard *everyone* would do it. The *hard* is what makes it great." He then spins on his heel and walks toward the bus to leave with the rest of the team. Enough said. It's true. You really can't add to that.

Let me give you a personal example from track and field. I'm a sprinter, competing nationally and internationally against the fastest people in the world in my age category. I compete against former Olympians, former college stars, and former world record holders. In the first race I observed at my first world championships, an 80 year old man ran a 200 meters in 30 seconds. That's averaging 15 miles an hour for an eighth of a mile! That's when reality sank in. This was not going to be anything like the regional meets I had been competing in all summer.

At the National Championships held in Chicago in 2012, I was one of the top-seeded athletes, expected to medal or possibly win the gold. The first race I observed at this meet also told me it was not going to be a stroll in the park. The guy who won the 100 meter dash had been on the Jamaican 2004 Olympic team. He won but he didn't set a record. I would later race one of the guys who *had* set the record.

There was a problem coming into the meet, however. I had damaged myself by over-competing and overdoing it in my final workouts. I had a medical condition commonly known as over-training syndrome. It can be serious. It can end your career, just like it did to Alberto Salazar, the man who was on his way to becoming our greatest marathon runner ever. Your body simply will not rebuild and strengthen after a workout. At best, it heals, but only slowly.

For three weeks straight, I had competed in two meets a week, winning gold in three events at each meet. I had virtually no competition on the West Coast, so I was treating races as workouts. Then, in an unfortunate communication with my coach, I ran a double workout 10 days prior to the first preliminary heat of the 400 meters. He came late to practice. In a debrief, I told him what I had done already. He thought I was telling him what I was planning to do. He set me out running a couple of fast 300s and then had me begin to hit each 100 meter segment of the race. It was to be my last hard workout before the tapering-off period. At the end of the second 100, I stopped. I couldn't do any more. My legs felt like they were on fire. When my coach and I figured out what had happened, a grim silence hung in the air.

The next evening, I called one of my other coaches who also happens to be a professor of medicine at the University of Washington. I told him that my pulse, normally in the 40s was now in the high 70s. I couldn't sleep well. I was having crazy dreams.

After hearing the history of how I did this to myself, he took a long pause and said, "Charles, this is serious. You may have really hurt yourself. Overtraining is…serious. It can be permanent," he repeated, trying to impress upon me the need for uncharacteristic restraint. He told me to do nothing until I got back to Chicago.

The high pulse and the horrible sleep continued for another week. But I decided to go to Chicago. On the day before the preliminary heats, I tried running just a bit. I chose to shut it down shortly after starting. I was still achy and miserable. But at least my pulse was down and I was able to sleep better.

Then a wonderful thing happened. On the day of my preliminary heat, the temperature soared to 98 degrees and the humidity became so thick, it was like being wrapped in a plastic bag. This was my break. The temperature on the track was going to be in 100s. Who on earth was going to do a full warm up in that kind of heat? It was going to be draining. It was going to be utterly miserable.

It was hard.

As a sprinter you have to warm up. Warming up is not intended to make your muscles warm. That's just a byproduct. It is intended to increase the amount of blood in your muscle tissue. Not by 30%. Not by 50%. But by one thousand percent! A good warm up will increase the usable blood supply to the muscle cells by 10 times. So, miserable as it was, hard as it was, I warmed up until I was red-faced, scorched, and sick to my stomach. I jogged a full mile and ran a 300 at 85%. I then did 100 after 100 after 100, followed by a hard set of strides and short sprints. I was all alone out there.

I won my heat by 30 meters. I was even able to shut it down and try to save some for the finals the next day. It was too late to repair all the damage but this day I had had more than enough in me to beat a lot of guys who did not warm up all the way. That night the high pulse and crazy dreams came back.

The next day I was racing a legend, Charles Allie. He had won his preliminary heat and I had won mine. I knew if I ran his race in the first 200 meters, I would further damage myself and not be able to finish the home stretch. The final straightaway of the 400 is the hardest 100 meters in the world of track and field. But those glorious hot and humid conditions persisted. Charles Allie and I were the only ones doing a full warm up.

I ran my own race, holding off a final stretch challenge by another competitor. He was a speedster, who later took the bronze in the 200. But in this 400, I got the silver. Charles Allie set an age-related record. I suspected something big had happened when the officials came up to him while he was still catching his breath and they whisked him off the track for a drug test.

He was recently selected as Masters Athlete of the Year for the whole planet. He'll receive his award in Monaco. He is an amazing competitor. And he always does the hard thing.

The <u>hard</u> *is* what makes it great. The <u>hard</u> helps eliminate most of your competition. All you have to do is hang in there and do what you're supposed to do and you'll be one of the winners.

That's where we are now in the corporate world – the American workplace. Morale stinks and the personal relationships between management and employees sometimes feels a bit like living in the DMZ between North and South Korea. It feels like an endless stalemate. Productivity is suffering because workers don't feel like engaging. The polls and studies show it's impacting turnover, absenteeism, product quality, customer satisfaction and, of course, market share and profits.

It's hard. That's what you want.

When it's hard, it always feels new and abnormal. It seems like there really isn't a clear way forward. There's certainly no formula. So people hunker down, emerging every once in a while to try new tricks like crazy employee perks or a charm offensive at the company picnic. But they can't conceive of an overall plan. And since the problem is affecting their competitors just as bad as it's affecting them, this Millennial thing must therefore be permanent, cultural, and insoluble. It is what it is.

That's the good news. The other guys have quit. They got in the car and drove off. They aren't warming up because it's 105 degrees on the track.

And you quit too. You quit doing normal things just like every other business did 20 years ago. The rest of this book will tell you what to do. But in the meantime…

Get out on there on the track and sweat and overheat for just 30 minutes. Your competition is sitting in the shade hoping the weather will change.

Chapter Seven
Initial Thoughts on Getting There from Here
(Secret IBM Investment Strategies)

Let's start with a few secrets from the guys who made life really hard for all their competitors. Think of this as your 30-minute warm up while the other guys are watching the thermometer.

IBM was a great company. I speak in past tense because now it's just a very, very good company, well run and successful. It quit being great the day they announced that the employee was no longer #1. As soon as you do something that misguided, you will no longer be #1. I will discuss this more in Chapter Eight, Still Tribal After 2 Million Years.

There were a lot of things IBM espoused. I've mention a number of them in this book. And then there were those things you had to observe – those little gems and secrets you discovered that made you say to yourself, "So that's the secret. That's how it works." There were lots of *secrets* I picked up because I was always paying attention to the nuances. As Yogi Berra once said, "You can observe a lot just by watching."

So let's follow a thread of ostensibly unrelated investment secrets that will very much relate to what we propose as a critical strategy for dealing with the issue of workplace discontent in the Millennial era. The first of these secrets came along when we sought to answer the question: which clients should we invest our increasingly limited sales resources into? What I learned eventually applied to so much more than resource allocation.

As computers grew more powerful, while getting smaller and more affordable, IBM was faced with the issue of how to cover all those potential clients. You can't assign a sales person to everyone who might buy a computer. At the same time, you don't want to miss the next Microsoft or Xerox that comes out of nowhere and suddenly becomes a giant.

So we turned to MIT and asked them to help us find the distinguishing characteristics of companies that were likely going to become great. As the project continued, it really came down to one thing that was a very solid differentiator: How do they respond to downturns in their business or downturns in the economy in general?

The companies that were going to pop up out of the pile of also-rans (the mice) to become what we called "gazelles" on the way to becoming elephants, all had a tendency to invest when things started turning down. When everyone else hunkered down or hid under their desk, they got aggressive and took market share.

To be safe, most companies will wait until the upturn has been underway for a while and then they'll start investing in their growth. But how does that work in the phony economy we have now? We are in a protracted slide with blips that occur on the graph every once in a while but are finer than frog hair. They get your hopes up but they don't last too long. So no one is investing in corporate infrastructure, right?

Here and there, someone out there is starting to invest and go after market share. They are increasing their sales force, expanding their product lines, adding new software and technology, training their people, rolling out new customer satisfaction programs. In a prolonged state of economic malaise, companies will eventually do all of these things, so no one will really pull ahead unless they do a bunch at once or really hit hard on the right one. So where are they not investing that they should be? Where might an investment be made that could spring the company forward, solve a bunch of problems, and take advantage of these Millennial era issues? That brings us to the next secret IBM investment strategy.

Where on your P&L is the line item for "management"? You have wages and employee benefits, executive comp, commissions, etc. But you don't have a single line item for managers. That's partly due to standard practices but it's also because companies don't think of managers as a separate class. They certainly don't think of it as an asset class where they are expecting a good return. They pretty much view it as overhead. They have to pay someone to babysit employees in groups of 8 to 15 or so. If you don't think of it as an asset and you *do* think of it as overhead, you are not going to invest in it, let alone measure ROI.

But that's not how IBM thought of management. True, it's a cost to be controlled but since you're spending a ton of money on it, you expect it to get a big return on what you are spending. You set high targets for them to hit and then you train them to hit those targets. You invest in management training and you never stop.

When the doldrums hit IBM in the late 80s and early 90s, this became a critical issue. We had always set high targets, now we had to control the costs even more tightly. We had to get more from fewer managers. What did we do? We reinvested in management training. We all had to go to transformational management classes. Among other things, we had to learn to focus more on what and a lot less on how. This allowed us to expand our span of control. A number of managers returned to non-management roles. We increased our customer coverage without increasing overall headcount. It was a smart move. What versus how sounds easy, but you need training.

The final secret IBM strategy is known outside of IBM as well. But is it practiced? Can you ensure it gets implemented?

The final secret is that you only hire A-players, because they are typically three to five times as productive as B-players but they don't cost three to five times as much. That's a great investment. But it too is not as easy as it sounds. What if A-players don't want to work for you? What if you have already hired a bunch of B-players? How do you tell the difference in performance for jobs that are not easily measured?

Answers to these is a book in itself. But quickly, you need to change who you are, create an exciting vision, become a secure place to work, and then people will want to work for you. If you don't do that, get out your checkbook and pay large amounts to buy some A-players. And if you have a lot of people who need to come up to speed, then invest in your managers and have them get everyone on a heavy development course, companywide.

Surprisingly, IBM found itself in the position of too many B-players as we rolled into the 90s. We were going to go from being a computer company to becoming a company that solved information problems. That meant we were going to go from just being hardware and software salespeople to also becoming systems integrators and project managers. A lot of people didn't make the cut. Formerly stellar, A-players were now B-players. The economics got away from us and we ended up laying off an awful lot of people. Our first layoff in history was an ugly one.

But even in this, I learned an interesting lesson. For more than a year prior to the layoffs, we were forced to rank our employees. We didn't suspect there was going to be a layoff, so we didn't put two and two together. Many people, including myself, fought the ranking process and were outspoken opponents throughout its implementation. Ranking any humans, but especially humans whose jobs are not identical, is vintage Industrial Revolution, people-as-means-of-production dehumanization. I was top-ranked in my category of manager and as a result I got a huge bonus each quarter. When asked how I felt after several of those bonuses, I offered to give them all back if we would stop ranking people. It was a hollow offer on my part but it expressed my sentiments.

When we did our ranking, we were required to do so based on a common set of attributes. We had to document this for each of our employees. We couldn't use the old lifeboat strategy, where you say who you would toss out first, second ... until there is only one left. We instead tried to standardize it.

When I looked at that list later on, I decided that is the list you should use in the first place, when you hire people. They were common attributes such as adaptability, flexibility, and communication skills. I took that list and expanded it. So now when I hire, I have two strategies: IBM's best athlete strategy and the strategy that asks who you would rather be stuck with on a deserted island in the middle of the Pacific. For the latter, it comes down to personal traits more so than specific skills. That person you would rather be stuck with is the A-player.

I teach this in my management development classes along with a bunch of other strategies including employment law issues. Hiring is complex and there needs to be a lot of people involved, including both genders on every hire. The hiring process is an investment in itself.

Companies today are facing a big problem in a tough economy. IBM was facing a big problem and we finally addressed it and got back on our feet. The sad news is that it took us 20 years and thousands of people being laid off to figure out how to do it. It is unlikely that most companies can spend even 5 more years figuring out how to deal with the sea change taking place, evidenced by the Millennial phenomenon and the attendant awful workplace environment. But at least you now have the three-step, secret IBM investment plan.

So invest during these tough times. Invest in training your managers. And then have your managers hire and develop only A-players.

Chapter Eight
Still Tribal after 2 Million Years

The failure to ignore how people are designed, despite abundant evidence, including our personal feelings and experiences, is a mistake that only humans could make.

For a long period of time, there was a model in the field of psychology, known as drive theory, which was introduced and developed in the middle part of the 20th century by Dr. Clark Hull. To simplify, it said that animals have what he called cravings for things such as food, water, and sex and that they try various ways to satisfy these cravings. Those ways that succeed are reinforced and become habits. In other words, we figure everything out from scratch.

He even took this to such lengths as to explain why mice fear cats. Here's how that works: A mouse with a food craving is sniffing around for grain and sowbugs when he gets the scent of something different. He looks up and sees a cat. The cat takes a vicious swipe at the mouse, gives it a good scratch and the mouse flees to one of its other cravings, safety. The next time the mouse smells or sees a cat, it knows that this is something to be feared.

Over time, Hull's theories and explanations got a bit clunky and were replaced by those of Skinner and others. All of them had at their basis the notion that we (members of the higher orders of the animal kingdom) enter the world pretty much as a blank slate and learn how to act via a series of reinforcement mechanisms.

One of my professors at the University of Washington, Dr. Robert Bolles, negated the Hullian drive theory. He asked some of us to proof a new book he was introducing and I took the opportunity to spend time with him to learn more. His theories fit more with my own theological notions that we were built in a fairly complete way and that circumstances modified what was in us to create a range of inherited human behaviors.

He was mostly focused on defense responses but still, it supported the theory that animals of even high cognitive capacity are born with some very complex behaviors they are predisposed towards under certain circumstances. The very first time that mouse scented a cat, it didn't have to come close to being killed to learn that cats are dangerous. Nor did it have to figure out what to do. It was pre-wired. Bolles called it an SSDR, a species-specific defense response.

We now know that very complex behaviors can be controlled by just a single gene pair. This was discovered when trying to figure out what was causing whole beehives to get diseased and die from what was known as American foulbrood disease. In this disease, dead larvae left in the hive breed bacteria that eventually kill all the bees. Oddly, it was found to be genetic.

A researcher crossed queens with male bees from two separate colonies, one afflicted by the disease, the other from a non-foulbrood hive. As is often the case with a recessive gene, the trait was not manifested in the offspring. But in crossing the sets of offspring, a curious thing happened. They found that one fourth of the bees had full blown foulbrood disease and one fourth had no indication of foulbrood whatsoever. But what about the other two fourths?

Here's where it gets interesting. In one of the four groups, when the worker bees detected a dead larva, they would unseal the wax from the cell it was in but they would just leave the larva there to rot. In the other fourth, if the researcher unsealed the wax cap of a dead larva's cell, the worker bees would pull out the dead larva, drag it outside of the hive, and toss it away. This proved that fairly elaborate sets of behavior can be stored in one gene pair, on one chromosome.

We have millions of genes. As humans got bigger and smarter, we also got relatively weaker and slower physically. We became more and more dependent on what was stored in our minds. We didn't have time to <u>learn</u> that saber-toothed tigers were unpleasant companions at the watering hole.

And we became more and more dependent on one another. Larger, probably more intelligent Neanderthals were wiped out by smaller statured, smaller brained Homo sapiens (us) about 50 thousand years ago. We banded together. They didn't. We thrived. They ceased to exist. This is still theory, but the evidence is getting far stronger with the new technology for DNA analysis.

Via mitochondrial DNA modeling, we also now suspect that the group of people that crossed over from northeastern Africa a hundred thousand years ago was probably less than 200 in number. Three conclusions can be drawn from this fact: we are very fortunate to have survived; we are all very closely related; and the combination of instinct and intellect we brought with us, worked very, very well.

So here's an idea: Now that we're safe from Neanderthals and large predatory felines, let's just forget how we are wired and start from scratch. Let's try the Hullian approach and see if we can't just try new tricks to redirect the "cravings" of individuals. Instead of being managers doing business, let's be manipulators running a new experiment every year, ignoring the last 2 million years of human existence that made us the way we are. Let's forget that we have learned to cling together, struggle for a common cause, develop individual worth via contribution to the whole, and trust our powerful, capable leaders to take care of us.

Let's play modern business!

Listen in on a conversation that might have taken place 40 thousand years ago. One of the tribal leaders is talking to one of the women who is making urns for water storage. You tell me if this ever could have happened.

Leader: Hi there, Nunu, I see you're back at it, making some more water urns.
Nunu: Yeah, my wrist is better and we have dry season coming, so I need to start making up some batches of clay.
Leader: Well, that's what I wanted to talk to you about. You see the last several batches you made had some thin spots and when the jugs got full, they cracked.
Nunu: I know that was a problem with the early batches but I thought they had gotten better. I'm really trying.

Leader: They haven't gotten that much better. And it turns out that all your trying doesn't keep water from spilling all over the ground, now does it?

Nunu: Well then, I'll just have to really watch closer so that...

Leader: Too late, Nunu. You're done.

Nunu: What should I do then? Should I make hide-cloths?

Leader: We have plenty of folks stitching leather, Nunu.

Nunu: Should I maybe make more bone needles so that more people can stitch hides? We ran low last winter on coats and boots.

Leader: Frankly, Nunu, nobody feels real good about the work you do. I don't think anybody would look forward to sewing up a swatch of mammoth hide with a needle made by you, knowing it might snap halfway through the process. I really think it's just time for you to leave the tribe.

Nunu: But there must be something I can do.

Leader: Let's not make this harder than it needs to be, Nunu. Take an extra handful of raisins and a couple good-sized strips of buffalo jerky and head off into the wilderness.

Nunu (crying): But where will I go?

Leader: Really not my problem. You'll figure something out.

It wasn't until the Industrial Revolution that people could come together as a group and then just simply get tossed out on a whim if they didn't meet the needs of the guys in charge. For the 2 million years prior to that, if you were part of the group, you were *permanently* part of the group. Only serious offenses could get you kicked out. Organized religion had excommunication and that was viewed as so horrendous that it pretty much kept everyone with their shoulder to the orthodox wheel. Fear of separation from the group is pretty awful.

Some say that feudal society prepared us for industrial age hierarchies and the destruction of individual rights. But that's just not true. People didn't get kicked out of feudal towns. They may have picked up bad names like the town fool but they stayed in town to practice their foolery.

In his excellent book, *The Crusades Through Arab Eyes*, Amin Maloof makes a fascinating observation. Most people don't really understand what took place in the Crusades. They think it was a bunch of knights and foot soldiers hopping on ships and attacking people in Palestine for a variety of reasons related to religion and greed. But what they don't know is that it involved the migration of tens of thousands of European commoners overland to the Middle East to live in the lands newly conquered by the West.

Ultimately, the European armies and the inhabitants of the towns they built were sent packing. After they were gone, here is what was observed by one Arab about the feudal system of rights. He noted that unlike the Arab system where only one person had all the power and all the rights, the European system had different layers of rights all the way down to the lowest level. These rights were inviolable. He felt that even the Arabs who lived in these towns missed such a concept when the Europeans left.

It turns out that the age-old Middle East system wherein one person has all the power and then loans it out to the next layer and so forth, is not natural. And it doesn't work. You can't compete with the natural order that vests rights to all inhabitants. One of these rights is permanent belonging and individual worth of some kind. People simply aren't expendable, nor can they be marginalized in a normal healthy society. The Middle East is unhealthy by almost all standards.

This notion of expendability is now everywhere. Look at what happens when someone messes up in our society. If a newscaster or other prominent media person says something politically incorrect, they get fired or permanently ostracized. We smell blood and we all react. "Get 'em!" By agreeing to pile on, we cravenly keep our own standing intact. We're sick. Culturally, we have a disease that is killing the whole hive.

I have been promoting this theme for some time now and it's resonating, especially with younger people. When I wrote *A Guide to Managing Earthlings*, I only briefly touched on this idea. However, the back of that book cover makes it very clear how I feel. I pointed out that IBM, my corporate alma mater, was a very compassionate company but that they didn't go far enough:

> *They ignored one critical element in our makeup. We are tribal creatures at heart. We want to belong to the group permanently. We want security and recognition of our work and our worth. We want our leaders to be competent and noble.*

We have dozens of social behaviors that we just do. We don't learn them. We simply do them. We talk to one another encouragingly. We collaborate for the sheer joy of working together. We divide up tasks and we're excited to bring back to the group the product of our labor. When someone does something great, we like to celebrate and encourage them to do more because we will likely all benefit.

We're constantly asking, "What's going on?" and "What are we doing next?" No one teaches us to be socially inquisitive.

We want to share what we have and it bothers us when someone else doesn't. It bothers us even more when we see someone struggling along who has very little and someone else who has more than they could ever use, consume, or in any way enjoy. It also bothers us a lot when we see so many people vying for power. It says we lack true leadership and we know instinctively that's dangerous.

We want to take care of our families and we assume everyone wants to take care of theirs. It's felt that people who are weaker should be dealt with more carefully. When someone is in pain, we should all come up with a way to ease the suffering.

In times of scarcity, we should all lighten our demands on the whole. And when all our good work and our good treatment of one another pays off or when it's just been an inexplicably great season of harvest, we should all share.

This isn't some phony idea of Utopia. This is us. We don't need to design a way to make us act like us. We don't need communism or state sponsored socialism with the inevitable rise to rule of the power-hungry who will create their own feudal system while spouting noble intentions. We here in capitalist America can do everything we ought to do if we just stay true to our design and our tribal roots.

But when we build corporate cultures that ignore our innate sense of how people should be treated, we create a mess. We then add to that mess by coming up with manipulative solutions that don't last. When morale once again sinks, it's assumed that the people must be fundamentally messed up. And now that we have Millennials behaving in ways we never did, we have "proof" they are fundamentally messed up.

Unfortunately, all the new tricks aren't working. But fortunately, the people are still reliably human, built and wired the way we have been built and wired for thousands of millennia – two thousand millennia, to be clear. The additional good news is that we find out very quickly in the Information Age that the latest tricks aren't working. So then what's the next trick?

How about no more tricks?

People are demanding humane management for humans because each new generation now brings ever stronger proof of who we were just two million years ago.

Chapter Nine
What Millennials Can Learn from Africa
(Because All Prior Generations Did Not)

It even existed when I was in Africa – this feeling that we European-types (including Americans) know just about everything and the indigenous Africans know nothing of any value. What is surprising is that this even extends to the topic of Africa itself. We know what's good for them on just about every front. And we often tell them so. But just as often, we go about our business smugly aware of the huge gap in "advancement" on just about every one of [our] measures of civilization and societal worth.

If you look at the scorecard, conveniently supplied by us, it pretty much makes the case. If you look at technological achievements, military prowess, advanced education, governmental sophistication, agricultural techniques, and operating infrastructure, the contrast between what we find in Africa versus what we have developed in the West has been pretty stark over the last couple of centuries.

Perhaps it was a good thing that when I walked into that remote Kenyan setting, the lone white guy in a village of 7000 Luo people, I was at a point in my life of some uncertainty. I was looking for answers and I didn't even know the questions. It was a village of mud huts, no electricity, no running water, no cars or equipment of any kind, bare feet, bad hygiene, and half the kids dying by age five. I had more technology inside my backpack than existed in all the rest of the village.

So why did I come home such a changed man?

Toward the end of my first book, *Breath of Kenya*, I wrote this as I flew from Nairobi on my way to Amsterdam:

> *My flight was scheduled for 11:35 PM. It was running late and I would not be taking off until after midnight. Passengers sat waiting for the plane in a grubby little gate area. There was standing room only. But something was different. I think it was me.*
>
> *One after another, babies began to cry. Soon eight were crying. Not long ago, even one crying baby would have irritated me and made me wonder why the mother wasn't doing a better job. Now, I just felt sorry for these mothers and their tired little babies. I wasn't the least bit irritated.*
>
> *Our flight went north through the Sudan and the lifeless Sahara. As we reached the shore of the Mediterranean I glanced back for as long as I could get an angle. I knew I would be back, whoever I now was. I say that because this was just too much. Death and sunshine, bloated babies and sugar cane groupies, dead Zebras, frightened bicyclists pumping rusty old bikes past tired young women in the middle of the night. All this was running through one fuse in my little white brain. It was just too much. It's still too much.*
>
> *I will never look at life the same way again.*

We know so little about Africa and even less about Africans. We're like cynics: We know the price tag of everything and the value of nothing.

I'm so grateful to those patient Kenyans who endured my "wisdom" until I could learn something from them. And what did I learn?

I learned that love is an action not a feeling and that it can permeate the whole day, spread across the entire village and be passed on from generation to generation without the word love ever being mentioned. Love is patient and kind and diligent. Tolerance isn't love.[19] It's non-love. But patience is.

I learned that you can give when you've got next to nothing. And there's plenty more where that came from because people don't want things. They want respect. And they want caring, which is another thing that's an action, not a feeling.

I discovered that the less you have, the better job you'll do of preserving it, while still sharing with others.

I found out that you've got to keep going when really bad stuff happens and you can't worry about anything because the stuff that gets you isn't the stuff you were worried about. All worrying does is show you how pathetic most of your priorities are.

I treated a lot of people for illnesses, many of which were life threatening, like gangrene and double pneumonia. I remember a woman handing me her two-year old daughter,

---

[19] I now view "tolerance" as worse than worthless. It's a pacification technique. The next time you feel like being tolerant of someone who's different from you, how about engaging with them like they're from the same planet? Take action. That's love; not phony PC tolerance.

sick and congested. The baby looked at me all steamy and listless. And then her eyes rolled back in her head. The mother asked me calmly, "Can you help her, Cha-lees?"[20]

You have no idea how this changed what I considered to be a big problem after I returned to America.

Okay, why am I telling you this and what does it have to do with Millennials – especially those who don't plan to go to Africa any time soon?

What I was doing before I caught on and what Europeans have done for the last several hundred years in Africa, is exactly what Millennials are doing today. And I think the consequences are going to be just as bad for them and for this country. I'm already seeing it.

Europeans were so much more advanced, by their every measurement, than the Africans that they simply felt they had nothing to learn from them. That had to do with the fact that what the Europeans valued most was progress, measured in purely material terms. Things. They liked things and more things. None of the "things" the Africans had were of any use other than as little showpieces for parties or decorations for their libraries.

So what salient artifacts do Millennials value and what do we Boomers have to offer them? On a day to day basis, it's kinda

---

[20] That was somehow my name in the village. I don't know where the "r" went.

looking like we Boomers offer nothing. If one's whole life centers around communication technology, gaming, and social media, then what does a group of people who are nowhere near as adept at those things have to offer to the group for whom such things are truly second nature?

I remember being 16 years old and just learning to work on cars when cars were a big thing. Detroit ruled. And you better know how to work on them because they broke down all the time. Young men in their teens and twenties were also very much into performance. Knowing how to get the most oomph out of your 4-barrel Holly carburetor was considered a valuable skill.

The guys who really knew their cars were looked up to. And despite any lack of formal education, their jargon-filled musings amid an otherwise desolate vocabulary made them seem like sages. What's more, their sagacity was not limited to cars. Because when you're the guru on the most important topics, you must also be the final authority on everything else. Their opinions on women, beer, politics, smoking, and other major topics of the day were pretty much the final word. If your opinion differed, it was best you keep it to yourself.

About that time, I read *Of Mice and Men* by John Steinbeck, a depression-era story that takes place mostly on a ranch where the two central characters had hired on as field hands. There was a passage that struck me because I had already observed and made a personal note of what I mentioned above about the unassailable wisdom of the best mechanics.

A tall man stood in the doorway. He held a crushed Stetson hat under his arm while he combed his long, black, damp hair straight back... He was a jerkline skinner, the prince of the ranch...capable of killing a fly on the wheeler's butt with a bull whip without touching the mule. There was a gravity in his manner and a quiet so profound that all talk stopped when he spoke. His authority was so great that his word was taken on any subject, be it politics or love. This was Slim, the jerkline skinner.

That's how it always is. And the guys in the know don't really want to know what you know.

We are in the age of a rapidly expanding knowledge base, with more new data and information created every 10 years than was accumulated in the prior 10,000 years. Seriously. They can actually measure it now.

But just as stored facts and factoids are compounding, I can hear the hiss of wisdom escaping from mankind, perhaps not as fast, but it's at least linear and possibly exponential. The old have always complained about the unwillingness of the young to listen and learn. There has always been the fear among the elderly that everything they've learned will die with them. So what's different now?

It comes down to technology. In past generations, the technical knowledge was held by the senior, more experienced among us. We depended on them to teach us and bring us along. Since they knew more about the essentials for getting through life, we listened to them on every other subject along the way. But that is no longer the case. The younger are technically ahead of the older and the gap is growing. The young no longer depend on those one or two generations ahead. They certainly don't respect them. The last thing they're going to do is listen to them on collateral subjects such as how the world works. Just as we chose not to listen to Africans who wished to share the collective wisdom of the generations of Africans as it pertained to Africa.

Europeans were unable to see past their technological superiority and Africa is the worse for it, despite roads, phone lines, and hydroelectric dams. We learned nothing because we thought there was nothing to learn. All that tribal wisdom - folklore with a basis, and sentiments expressed without words - all but gone forever.

Millennials, you need to look past the technology. That gray-haired iPhone klutz might actually know something. Listen to him, even if he doesn't sign onto Facebook more than once every leap year. Every one of us who went before you knew by the end of our first year of college that we had all the answers. We knew the world would be a lot better and certainly a lot more fun with a socially lax and morally promiscuous set of standards.

But because we were forced to grow and we were dependent on those who went before us, we were forced to listen and gradually we learned. Millennials will be the first generation that will not have to grow up until well into their 40s and they are certainly not dependent on Generation X, let alone Baby Boomers. They don't have the safeguards of society that we resented but now know we really needed.

So, Millennials, will you listen to us *Africans*?

Chapter Ten
How Millennials Are Forcing the Inevitable

What do you as a boss do when the people you threaten are no longer afraid of being fired? What do you do when bluster and intimidation don't work or when the last batch of crazy perks you picked up from a business magazine aren't pumping up morale like you hoped?

It is my contention that old-style management techniques are going to continue to yield unsatisfactory results to all parties. We are soon going to be given a choice: manage humanely or get used to high turnover and worse. What could be worse? How about a zombie workforce that doesn't even see the point in quitting a job they hate because they know the grass isn't any greener elsewhere?

Are Millennials forcing the inevitable? And what do I mean by "the inevitable?" The answer is yes. And here's what I mean by it.

Human Axiom #1
We are genetically wired to treat one another within our tribe in a way that is mutually beneficial and ultimately in the best interest of the tribe.

Going along with that is the following:

Corollary to Human Axiom #1
When we are not treated in a way that is mutually beneficial, we know it, instinctively. It hurts and we resent it.

When people attain power via wealth or they attain power via appointment by another powerful person it can and usually does lead to abuse of that power. The statement by Lord Acton, a historian back in the late 1800s is true:

Power tends to corrupt and absolute power corrupts absolutely.

This is his most famous quote but there is another of his quotes that is worth examining. And, while they are aimed at government, they apply to our discussion of managing in a Millennial world.

The danger is not that a particular class is unfit to govern. **Every class is unfit to govern.** *The law of liberty tends to abolish the reign of race over race, of faith over faith, of class over class.*

The problem is no one likes to be governed. They want freedom. The difference between this generation versus every other generation that has previously entered the workforce is that Millennials *expect* it.

"But, Charles," you say, "business is not a democracy." My response to that is, "Sorry, pal. That ship has sailed."

People today believe to some extent that they should have a say in everything and that the power of those in authority ought to be limited to some extent. That, my friends, to a greater or lesser extent, is American democracy.

The toothpaste is out of the tube and you're not going to stuff it back in – not with edicts, swagger, or charm.

Previously I mentioned the book, *Generation Me* by Jean Twenge. -well worth the read to understand the Millennial mindset. She makes the case that one element of that mindset is the belief that many of the people in positions of authority don't deserve to be there. Millennials believe that certain people just happened to be standing there when the manager job came open. They got there first. Position and relationships got them their job, not merit. They believe this goes on throughout the company therefore almost no one is *fit* to manage.

So you have a bunch of people with a tendency to abuse power which a second bunch of people don't think the former bunch should possess in the first place.

Do you see where this is headed? It can go one of two routes: The malaise and chaos route or the collegial, fellow-tribesman route. The former has been a miserable, 300-year long experiment of the industrial revolution and the latter a temporarily interrupted standard of humankind for the last two million years. Given the momentum, which one are you going to bet on?

There are two other traits that have persisted amongst us humans for at least two million years: people will follow actual leaders and they enjoy being part of egalitarian groups.

In their book *Sex at Dawn*, the authors Christopher Ryan and Calcilda Jethá make a strong case for the utter egalitarianism of hunter gather tribes. With both land and material possessions being nonexistent, power plays are not only unnecessary, they can hurt everyone in the tribe. When the hunt is complete, everyone shares.

Only when agriculture came into play 8000 to 10,000 years ago, was land ownership and everything that went with it an important part of existence. You had to have land to grow stuff. That led to wealth accumulation and wealth disparities. Control of accumulated wealth and the desire for more wealth led to power struggles and organized governments with armies and hierarchies.

If you think I'm about to recommend Communism, complete with five-year plans and changing the name of employee to comrade, you couldn't be more wrong. Putting the power to decide wealth control and management in the hands of the politburo just leads to hierarchies and bureaucracies composed of individuals with even less merit and no right to hold power.

But we cannot escape two factors: People are wired to be collegially egalitarian and Millennials are demanding it. Maybe I should toss in two more: The present system is slowly failing and there are 82 million Millennials in the USA alone.

One other interesting fact that is discussed in *Sex at Dawn* has to do with group size. It seems that once you get more than about 150 people with whom you can identify, the sense of belonging rapidly goes away. Along with it go all the little social mechanisms we employ to keep one another in check, such as shaming into compliance someone else in your disconnected mega-tribe who is a selfish jerk.

Does that mean you should never have a corporation with more than 150 employees? No. Here's what it means:

1. You must take extraordinary actions to make people feel connected.

2. Every subgroup must have a very clear sense of purpose – a reason to exist – that is shared by every member of the group.
3. The purpose of that subgroup must be obvious in its direct linkage to the corporate mission as a whole.
4. Within that subgroup the people must feel like the person in charge is a true leader and that their peers are true peers. Everyone must feel that they will be heard when the need arises.

All of the above comes down to execution. And that comes down to managers who are trained to execute in the modern world. But as we all know, we don't train managers anymore. We appoint them and hope it works out with our precious assets – our employees.

It helps if the people in the subgroup understand the company's mission, see the vision, and respect the person leading the corporation. It will make for a much more effective corporation. But it's actually not necessary for unit morale and it's certainly outside of the control of the individual unit manager. Getting all groups lined up and functioning well together is a matter of orchestration, which I cover in *A Guide to Managing Earthlings*.[21]

In the meantime, it will take some seriously different thinking on the part of management. It will take us to the point where all great changes occurs – the counterintuitive.

---

[21] Covered in Section 3 Operational Management and in particular in Chapter 10 "The Transmission of What," which discusses how to avoid the phenomenon of organizational parallax.

But before I do that, let me leave you with the prime directive for any organization, based on a combination of Human Axiom #1 (we're wired to treat other members of our tribe decently) and the fact that we tend to lose our tribal sense when the group is larger than 150. You must understand that in true hunter-gatherer tribes, not only is there a 100% collegial, egalitarian atmosphere, there is another element that is dictated by necessity. It is almost entirely non-punitive.

Not only is it foolhardy to harm or be at odds with a permanent member of your own tribe, someone you eventually will depend on, it is highly unproductive to have people spending any time whatsoever thinking about their own security, looking over their shoulder, or involved in intrigue.

But beyond productivity, it hurts. It's miserable. It causes humans to suffer. We do this to each other and we call it business; like that excuses it and explains away the pain.

So here's the Prime Directive:
Regardless of the size of the organization, we must create an entirely non-punitive, collegial environment and act as if we are all going to be together as one tribe, forever.

It will be hard to do this in a punitive nation that has 5% of the world's population and 25% of the world's inmates. But you can examine your own role as a manager, coach, teacher, etc. You can take a look at your carrot-and-stick approach and make one simple decision: toss out the stick.

Sidebar
When Millennials Finally Start Voting...

We should be emphasizing the Golden Rule at work and just about everywhere else. But something sinister is getting in the way of that. Slowly, our behavior is being regulated and therefore dictated by the government. This nation was founded on a healthy distrust of government. Now, it is run by a government that does not trust us.

It is my belief that Millennials who now are highly liberal as a group, will come to realize that they are losing their freedom. They will then face a really tough dilemma: vote for the guys who promote state-sponsored social equality or vote for the guys who want the state to play less of a role in all aspects of their lives. The problem is, they will never be presented that clean of a choice. They'll have to figure it out. And the more the government intrudes in their lives and spies on them, the more likely they are to vote for a new style of politician altogether.

Millennials don't think in terms of the Golden Rule. Half of them couldn't tell you what it is. But they do believe in live and let live. That's how they're going to vote in the future. It will either be for limited-government Republicans who have quit trying to legislate morality or it will be for socially conscious Democrats who work to dismantle the hideous regulatory system they've been building while trying to accomplish a safe, open and equal society.

I mentioned Lord Acton, the British historian who said "Power tends to corrupt and absolute power corrupts absolutely." He would be horrified by how far American democracy has traveled in that corrupting direction. Who did he think should rule? I'll repeat his answer, given in the previous chapter:

> *The danger is not that a particular class is unfit to govern. <u>Every class is unfit to govern</u>. The law of liberty tends to abolish the reign of race over race, of faith over faith, of class over class.*

But he said something that was more important and almost prophetic. The first part of this next quote, made in 1862, sounds exactly like what politicians are pushing today and the second part of the quote is the only answer.

> *Whenever a single definite object is made the supreme end of the State, be it the advantage of a class, the safety of the power of the country, the greatest happiness of the greatest number, or the support of any speculative idea, the State becomes for the time inevitably absolute. Liberty alone demands for its realization the limitation of the public authority, for liberty is the only object which benefits all alike, and provokes no sincere opposition.*

For those who have written off Millennials, don't. Living in the age of instant information, they are the last hope that people will rediscover the unique American formula before it's simply too late.

Chapter Eleven
The Humane Treatment of Earthlings
(An Extract from *A Guide to Managing Earthlings*)

If you think about it, acting humanely means not behaving in the way a human would often respond in a particular situation.

Frequently, when I teach a class on management, I get fired in role-play situations where I am playing the part of a "bad" employee. In one particular case, which you'll read about later in the book, I probably deserve to be fired by most companies' standards. I make it easier by being in-your-face obnoxious along with some other serious character flaws. We all feel kinda bad about squashing a harmless crane fly. You could have just cupped it in your hands and tossed it out the door. But when we smash a whining, blood-sucking mosquito, we celebrate. And in the office when we give a jerk what he deserves, it feels a lot better than when we really work over a harmless introvert that just can't seem to do the job very well.

But the "bad" employee gives us the opportunity to show our humanity – to him and to everyone else. We can show grace (the giving of something good that is undeserved) and mercy (the withholding of punishment that is deserved). These are godly characteristics, not naturally felt by us humans and certainly easily overcome by expediency when we get into positions of power.

We as executives and managers can change the world. If we don't do it, somebody else will. And that might not be good.

There are two great equalizing forces: social imperative and government. This book is not about sociology or governmental politics. It's about business management. But an underlying theme is the issue of humane treatment of our fellow citizens. It's about down-to-earth, practical management. If you are not a good manager, your people will suffer either directly as a result of your ineptness or as a result of the behaviors you adopt as a coercive taskmaster who cannot lead out of respect but must instead employ manipulation, threats, or perpetual maneuvers to be likable and popular. This book will teach you to manage out of competence which is at its most fundamental level solving the right problems the right way. First what and then how.

If you are a competent manager, you possess one of the two characteristics required for humane management. The other is caring. You simply must care. I was an executive who honestly cared, yet I hurt more people than I should have because I didn't adopt caring as an overarching principle that governed my every decision. It was a casual byproduct of my upbringing and experiences in life. I should have cared for the sake of caring.

Instead, I fired people I should have fired but could have found an alternative to doing so. I pounded on people who were more or less helpless to fight back, just like a tyrant. I withheld opportunities and beneficial treatment from people whom I didn't like – though often for good reason. And in so doing, I spread a wave of hurt to their families and to other humans who came into contact with them. Yet I was viewed as a great guy, by most people.

I remember firing a middle-aged man and sending him home in the middle of the afternoon to tell his wife they no longer had an income. I felt lousy. I wondered how long this lousy feeling would last. I fired him essentially to solve a business problem – my problem. And then I created a personal problem – my problem. But what about that guy and his wife? How did he respond when his wife looked at him and said, "What are we going to do?" My feelings were focused on me, once I had made the decision. Instead, they should have been focused on him (and her!) before I made that decision. In looking back, I could have come up with an alternative but I didn't. I didn't have to. I had the power with very few constraints.

It is time we constrained ourselves, unnaturally. Granted, a business is not legally a democracy. We businesspeople, especially we alpha males, look down on egalitarianism and meekness. But to some extent they need to be practiced by us. We need to get out in front of this trend in society. It's not going away. That's the practicality of it. And a better system of sharing while exercising meekness needs to be practiced by us because it's right. That's the humanity of it.

We leaders need to view ourselves as the head of a tribe because our employees view themselves as members of a tribe, instinctively. They don't want to see themselves as replaceable parts in some organic machine. When we treat them that way, we hurt not only them but everyone around them because we disrupt an instinctive, tribal sense of what should be. Any short-term gain achieved by removing that one part is greatly outweighed by the systemic damage done by creating an environment that is not secure for all. That's the practicality *and* the humanity of it.

Still, doing something inhumane often seems to have immediate advantages; even though when everyone does so, it produces the kind of awful morale and high (70% according to Gallup) degree of employee disenfranchisement that exists in today's work environment. It's a case of the fire in the theater. Here's how that works:

You're sitting in a crowded theater when a fire breaks out. You have a choice: do you walk to the exit in a calm and orderly fashion or do you run for the exit? Unfortunately, it turns out that everyone else has that same choice. So, it comes down to you individually versus them collectively. There are four possible decision alternatives for the theater group, you included. If you walk and they walk, you have a reasonable but not certain chance that you will live. If you run and they run, you all will smash into a big bunch at the exit and you will likely not survive. And if they all run and you just walk, you as an individual will almost certainly die. There is one other possible alternative. If everyone else will calmly walk toward the exit and you run as fast as you can, arms flailing, knocking old ladies aside, you will almost certainly survive. This is *your* best alternative.

This is not unlike what we are faced with in society and, closer to where I'm taking this conversation, in the workplace. If everyone else will just act like it's one big tribe, maybe you as an individual can fire people left and right and pound on "bad" employees and get away with it. You run while all the other manager's stifle their instincts and walk.

But I'm telling you, it doesn't work that way. In the theater emergency, we aren't worried about morale and that crowd's long-term willingness to continue to attend the theater. In the workplace, we should be worried about that but for the last twenty years, we seem to have stopped worrying. We don't train our managers to overcome their base instincts. In fact, we don't train them at all. So they are base and marginally competent when it comes to managing our most precious resource, our fellow human beings. If you don't have a sense of humanity, at least have an awareness of ROI and invest in that very expensive line item – your management team.

It's amazing what you must do to your operating procedures, your management policies, and your day-to-day communications when you commit to a policy to "First, do no harm," as Hippocrates instructed doctors so long ago. In addition to not being able to fire people except in rare instances, you can't lay off workers except for survival reasons, and you must create an environment where people want to show up every day and further the tribe's purpose, thus ensuring the likelihood of both thriving and surviving.

So now what are you going to do? Maybe you need to recognize that there will be lean times and get your people's skills up to where they need to be, including your managers. Perhaps you will also recognize that a whole bunch of your employees are less than perfect and you need to have both a plan for that fact as well as an attitude that will make the best of it. You will have to make that not-so-fine distinction between what you are allowed to do and what you should do. Sure, you can berate an employee in front of others and get away with it. But you should bite your tongue, decide if this situation even warrants a discussion, and then have a professional conversation, one on one, behind closed doors. [*A Guide to Managing Earthlings*] will show you how. It turns out that the best way to have good personal relationships with your employees is to de-personalize the management process and make discussions about performance both objective and collegial.

You can also be a moody SOB and your employees will just have to put up with it and try to time your mood swings. Or you can recognize that such behavior is both hurtful to people and harmful to business and keep your mood swung over to only one side of the positive-negative meter. You can guess which one. At IBM we didn't have to guess. It was written into each manager's performance plan: *"You will be upbeat at all times."* Moody managers didn't stay in management long. Your bad moods have a ripple effect that extends all the way to your people's spouses and kids. IBM wanted your mood positive because it's good business. I'm saying do it because it's what humans are supposed to do when they honestly care.

[*A Guide to Managing Earthlings*] can go a long way toward teaching the art of professional management and help make you a better leader. But at best it can only make a plea for you to care about your people, including the offensive ones and the ones that "deserve to be culled" from the tribe.

I once personally witnessed a woman being kicked out of a tribe in rural Africa. It was gruesome. She had no place to go. A big, strong woman, she wept uncontrollably and sobbed in huge spasms as she was pushed along and jeered at by the crowd. I can't go back and fix that and neither can anyone else. I can't go back to that woman who asked her husband, "What are we going to do?" – that husband I sent home without an income one afternoon. But you and I can go back to our tribes with a renewed sense of humanity and an overarching belief that we must care even if we feel just the opposite. That's what professionals do and that's what the most humane earthlings do because caring is ultimately an act, not a feeling. We all have had people who cared for us when they probably didn't particularly *feel* like it. We should pay that forward without trying to keep score. Our parents, our teachers, our coaches, and often our neighbors and friends have fulfilled their roles unilaterally, thank God. We will likely never be in a position to repay them. Now, as we assume this most intimate and impactful role as managers, we can in effect honor their decency by simply treating others the way we would want to be treated.

I actually wrote this chapter last for *A Guide to Managing Earthlings*. And while I'm neither a softy nor a bleeding heart, I have learned after a few decades of leading Earthlings, that true caring will greatly amplify all the hard-hitting management practices that follow in the rest of the book. Don't just feel it. Commit to it and do it. Your business will flourish and your employees will thrive.

Chapter Twelve
So, Here's What You Do

In Praise of the Counterintuitive
(And how we are always surprised
when new thinking works)

Think back on anything you ever learned to do that was difficult and really required lessons. Whether it was sports, music, or military maneuvers, what you thought you should do was very different from what your instructor told you to do. That's because the instructor's objective for any action is just slightly different than your objective.

When you grasp a golf club as a kid, your purpose is to a) hang on to it so it doesn't come out of your hands when you swing, and b) position your hands in such a way that you can really get all your arm power into whacking that ball. And then the instructor makes you lock down your pinky finger, rotate your palm on top of the grip, keep your left arm straight, and pull the club back slowly, while putting your weight on your feet in a way that you believe will only restrict your all-out power smash.

And what's with that backhand in tennis? Turn my back? Point what at what? Aw forget it. Just let me hit the ball.

"So, tell me again, Sergeant, when someone starts shooting at me, we get down and move *toward* where the bullets are coming from? Isn't that guy with the machine gun making it clear he would like us to go in the *other* direction?"

My very first boxing lesson was full of all kinds of counter-intuitive stuff. After having me spar with one of the more experienced kids, my coach called me out of the ring and told me to wait while he went to his office. He returned with two flat, folded paper lunch bags. He then explained as he tapped me on top of the head, "Charles, your head is right here on top of your neck, which is right in the middle of your body." He then held one hand way out to his side, "Your head's not waaaaayyyy out here. And it's not waaaaaayyyy out here," he showed me with his other hand. "They can't hit you in the back and they can't hit you below the belt. And if they're stupid enough to hit you on top of the head, let 'em."

He slapped me lightly on my lower abdomen with back of his hand and said, "You can cover from here to just above your eyebrows with only your forearms. And I'm going to have you prove it to yourself."

He then took one of the folded bags, put it on the side of my ribcage and told me to pin it down with my elbow. He did the same thing to the other side of my body. My job was to block the many, many punches he was about to throw at me without letting the paper bags slip to the floor. I did okay for a bit but then he stopped me and told me I only need to block one punch with one hand and to quit moving my hands like they were lashed together because it left me vulnerable to his other hand. Besides, eventually I was going to have to throw a punch myself.

This felt awkward and frustrating. Eventually I had to learn not to lean back when someone threw a haymaker but to lean in, bob and weave. If someone with long arms came along, I wasn't to stay out of reach I was to get in there. All of a sudden, being able to be a tight little ball of brutality, throwing compact punches that came mostly from my hips, while covering and keeping my chin down, made a lot of sense. In fact, it made more sense than lying on the canvas staring up at the lights, peaceful as that sounds.

I didn't stay in boxing long. It seemed like a good way to get hurt. That was about the only intuitive thing I brought to and from the sport. Mostly, I didn't want to be around the people who were in it. My trainer was nice enough but the guys that were in the group all seemed to have a lot of problems they were working on besides the "sweet sport" of boxing.

The nice thing about boxing is that when you make mistakes, you are immediately reminded of what you should have done. It feels bad and it sounds like this, "One, two, three, four…"

What does it sound like when we act like modern day bosses and mistreat our employees? You can't hear it? That's not uncommon. So, why don't I let you listen in on the conversation that takes place when your employee gets home? His son is waiting for him on the front porch.

Employee's Kid: Dad's home! Hey dad, can we play catch? I think I'll know how to throw a curve ball this time.

Your Employee: No, I'm sorry, son. Not tonight. I'm not feeling real good right now. I think I just want to rest and talk to your mom for a while.

That's not the sound of someone who is physically tired. That's the sound of someone who isn't sure about the future. He isn't sure if he can keep doing this but in today's lousy economy, he probably has to. And besides, where's he going to go? Is it going to be better anyplace else, regardless of the economy?

He hasn't heard anyone say "Thanks!" or "Good job!" in a long time. But he has heard someone tell him that the report he just turned in had a typo on page 3. He has heard his boss tell him in front of all his fellow employees that his suggestions in the meeting weren't well thought through, after interrogating him to show him how dumb he is compared to the boss. For punctuation, his boss rolled his eyes for all to see.

He hasn't heard anything about where the company is heading and how he fits in. He doesn't have a written career plan and has no idea what the boss thinks his strengths are that can be built on and developed further for the next potential assignment. He's never heard his boss ask, "What would you like to do next?" As far as the employee's concerned, he's not sure there even is a "next." No one asks him his opinion on anything.

Here's an interesting fact related to the above kind of management treatment: The people who hate it the most and who are the most unhappy with it are Baby Boomers. But they are not the most likely to quit when the economy gets better or there's another job opportunity elsewhere. The one who is more likely to quit – five times more likely, in fact – is the Millennial. They simply won't put up with it. Why is that?

It's simple. We Boomers were conditioned to believe that our lives were to revolve around the company. We were to adapt our lifestyle to the needs of the job. As kids, there were about 30 of us for even the crummiest jobs that were available, let alone the cool jobs like lifeguard or box boy at the grocery store. If we didn't adapt, there were at least 29 other Boomer kids who would.

Hiring Boss: You'll need to be here 10 minutes after school gets out and you'll work until 9 pm.
Boomer Kid: Yes, sir. No problem, sir. I'll run all the way here.
Hiring Boss: And there won't be any vacation.
Boomer Kid: Not planning any.
Hiring Boss: And there won't be any breaks, including bathroom breaks.
Boomer Kid: I won't need a break. And I won't drink any water and I'll swallow two tablespoons of salt so I won't need to go to the bathroom.

Of course, once you got the job you deeply regretted all those concessions – until you collected your $1.65 an hour, at which point you felt a little better. Over time, regret turns to resentment and resentment turns to bitterness. Bitterness makes you cynical. Soon, your hand is perpetually on the doorknob. But as a Boomer, you don't turn it.

Do you see how many steps the Millennials just saved? They went right from being hired to putting their hand on the doorknob without all that intermediate psychology. They have to care about you to resent you. And since you have made it clear from day one that you are in no way committed to them and in only the most superficial way do you care about them, they're just not going to get all worked up. It's akin to cynicism and chronic cynicism is a low-energy state.

So, what do we know and what do we do?

We know that it's not happy out there. We know that genetics are involved but not some new genetics that popped up in the people born in the 80s. We're dealing with 2 million year old chromosomes and the angle on bending that gene pool to fit our management style has been tried and found wanting by some pretty nasty industrialists for over two hundred years.

We know that what we're doing right now isn't working; so it's probably going to require some new thinking – something counterintuitive. Here's the good news, it's already been figured out. We built the case logically and decided that we are going to have to resort to humane management and treating people the way we should have been treating them all along. We are going to toss in as a check-and-balance measure the concept of treating others the way you would want to be treated. We'll start with the fundamentals and then we'll go to the specifics.

Here are the three fundamental, counterintuitive concepts:
1. Depersonalize the management process to improve personal relationships with employees
2. Employers must show their commitment first – not the employee
3. To the extent reasonable, adapt to the employee's lifestyle

Item 3 is where we'll really get specific but let's start with the first one, depersonalizing the management process to improve personal relationships with all employees but especially Millennials.

There is a fundamental concept taught in my book *A Guide to Managing Earthlings:*

Here's the rule:
The best managers deal primarily in business issues and not personalities.

You have got to get to the point where you can objectively discuss an employee's performance. This can only happen if they trust you. You have to get to the point where offering a criticism isn't an attack or a setup. It's got to be impersonal, whereby you take the performance item in question and talk about it in a collegial manner. You say things like, "Lisa, we had hoped to be a little further along at this point. What's getting in your way and is there anything I can do to help you succeed?"

If you have built a trust relationship wherein the employee believes you are working in their best interest, you can have this conversation repeatedly. If you have demonstrated nothing in the way of loyalty or commitment, if you have spent very little time talking about where Lisa's opportunities for career success lie, and if you have never bent her way in a tough personal situation, then good luck ever having a decent conversation. You're just a boss and you deserve some degree of disdain.

Let's see if we can start moving you into the category of a caring, respected, collegial manager in step 2:

Employers must show commitment and loyalty first

When I have made this comment in groups of executives, you can see a visible stiffening throughout the crowd. Here's what they are thinking:

"What do you mean show my commitment first!? I just hired them, offered them a good salary, and gave them a good place to work with some excellent benefits. Now I'm supposed to show my commitment!? Charles, tell me something; were you a hippie in the 70s or one of those weather underground guys?"

I was neither. There's simple logic behind my assertion. But let me first use the classic example showing the distinction between commitment and its poorer cousin, involvement. In order for someone to serve you a plate of ham and eggs, the chicken had to get involved but the pig had to commit.

When a manager in a big company and a prospective employee come to terms and the employee gets hired, who is the pig and who is the chicken? Does the manager shake hands and then call home and have this conversation? "Honey, could you go to the bank and transfer some funds? I just agreed to hire someone. I know this means that we probably won't be able to take that vacation we were planning and now Skippy is going to have to go to a State university instead of a private college but hiring this employee is the right thing to do."

Or did he just use up one of his hiring slots? Big deal.

The employee on the other hand is going to change his or her life in a lot of ways. They are choosing your company over all other opportunities. They will adopt your policies. They are adjusting their lifestyle and putting their trust in you to pay them fairly, treat them well, and hopefully give them some dignity and a chance to grow. If they are a Millennial, they will be looking for some purpose in what they do and will assume that to the degree possible, their job will be meaningful. They will not know until they show up and start working there if you will be able to honor that. They will just have to trust you.

The most stable figure in plane geometry is a triangle. But the most stable figure in solid geometry is a tetrahedron, which kind of looks like a pyramid. It is comprised of 4 equilateral triangles. Put on each face the names: Trust, Commitment, Loyalty, and Caring. In this you'll have the basis for a fabulous relationship. If you wait for the employee to show his or her loyalty before you show your commitment, the trust will disappear. You'll be back to a 2-dimensional, planar figure, which, in case your geometry teacher never told you, is not real. Stiff a Millennial on any one of the faces of the tetrahedron and they'll prove it's not real.

Francis Bacon once told a story (unfactually) in his *Essays*, saying that Mohammed was about to offer prayers before the people. He wanted to do it from the top of a hill. So in front of all the people he called the hill to come to him. After several attempts it was pretty clear the hill wasn't budging. So Mohammed supposedly said, "If the hill will not come to Mahomet, Mahomet will go to the hill." This scene is fictitious. It appears nowhere in Islamic canon or tradition. But evidently it sounds like a good idea to a lot of modern day managers to keep trying and not give up like Mohammed. They want the mountain of employees to abandon their collective humanity and come to them. And for 200 years, it sort of looked like it was working.

How's it looking now?

Let's look at the third counterintuitive fundamental:

> *To the extent reasonable, adapt to their lifestyle*

Once again, let's go back to one of the fundamental rules, in fact the pervasive theme of *A Guide to Managing Earthlings:*

Here's the rule:
Managers should focus on <u>What</u> almost exclusively and let their employees focus on <u>How</u>.

If you are primarily concerned with what gets done, a lot of the cosmetics and collateral stuff really won't matter. As a manager, you have tons of flexibility. As a supervisor neither you nor the employee has much room at all. Supervisors are *How* guys. Nobody wants a *How* guy.

Let's look at some adaptations and you tell me which ones are impossible or so important for you to say no to that you are willing to risk having a disenfranchised employee base.

1. **Allow flexible hours/flexible venue.** Just make sure the job is getting done and that they honor your trust. Communicate regularly but meaningfully. Tighten up when it starts feeling disconnected. There's not much space between disconnected and disenfranchised.

2. **Help build their resume. And tell them you're doing it.** This is important. Your company is part of their career – not the other way around. If they are looking to build new skills, help them do so. Give them the experiences they are looking for if you possibly can. They fear and loathe being underutilized, a condition rampant in today's workplace.
3. **Minimize formal meetings.** And get better at running the ones you do hold. Millennials can't stand a lot of meetings. They collaborate naturally. Go sit in on a gaming session where they're building things for each other all the time. Get on SharePoint or some other software that encourages ongoing sharing electronically. And then meet only when you have to or when it's fun.
4. **Minimize measurements and only review the big ones and exceptions.** Nobody wants to be bugged about the little stuff. Keep it simple and meaningful.
5. **Make appraisals uneventful and positive.** I'm not talking about the new style of powder-puff appraisals. If you have done a decent job of developing a collegial working relationship, and if you have been communicating all along, then you should be able to discuss just about anything.[22]
6. **Get their input constantly without going the consensus route.** Consensus managers are weenies. I'm not talking about going that route. Just get their input

---

[22] Old IBM rule: Performance appraisals are strictly for performance. Don't mix missions and talk about raises or careers. It can get messy. You can talk about those items in separate meetings and refer back to performance if necessary. Besides, who's listening to performance stuff if pay is about to be discussed?

before you make a big decision. Make it clear who owns the decision but at least hear what they've been thinking about - probably for a long time. They care. And they care to be heard.

7. **Overlook the small stuff – and most of it is small stuff. Make it clear they can make mistakes.** Don't talk about mistakes unless they are mission critical or are hurting the employee. Save them for a separate discussion if you're reviewing their work. If you start by pointing out the typo on page 3, they will hate you. In fact, I'll hate you. And I don't even know you.

8. **Support their charitable endeavors.** Why not? A lot of companies do matching grants. Millennials are very cause-oriented. To the extent that your company can be part of their lifestyle, do it.

9. **Constantly invest in their education.** Even if it's not directly job related. You become their career and resume hub. Why would they lightly give that up?

10. **Mentor purposely and specifically.** I find Millennials to be very open to someone who they feel is acting in their best interest and/or cares about them. If you don't like their Millennial manners or dress, if you think they talk unprofessionally or act in a way that you think is impacting their effectiveness, tell them. Point it out as gently as you would want it done to you and then hear their side.

11. **Listen to their ideas for you and the company.** They aren't a cog in your organic machine. At least, they don't think they are. They have lots of ideas. Keep 'em comin'. One of them may save your career someday. You don't have to adopt all their ideas. I can't tell you how many

times I have returned to a "crazy" idea 6 months later and modified it to fit a need. People want to feel heard. If they don't feel heard by you, they will go find someone else who will make them feel heard. People will talk until they feel heard. So be the guy they talk to.

12. **Make it clear that you believe in them as human beings.** This starts with caring and ends by being competent in your management. It means getting very good at the three utility functions of management: Communication, Delegation, Recognition of Performance – and doing them every day.

How hard was that list to understand? What looks undoable on it? Probably nothing. So go do it.

Let me finish with one more counterintuitive fundamental, which should be obvious but usually isn't.

> *The role of managers, from the CEO down to the first line manager is, first and foremost, to <u>serve.</u>*

All the way down the line, managers should be serving the people who ultimately serve the customers. This has always been true back to the days of kings and the Patriarchs. It was almost always ignored by dictators and tyrants. But that didn't make the rule less valid. In fact, it made it more achingly, obviously true.

If you have a servant's heart, you will have one of the necessary attributes, making you fit to lead any generation in any age.

Concluding Thoughts
A strategy for the next 1000 years

Successfully managing in the Millennial era or any era, for that matter, still ultimately comes down to two fundamentals: Competence and caring.

Competence requires training and experience. My book, *A Guide to Managing Earthlings* is intended as a source of experience-based instruction with lots of rules based on my own IBM training but with a significant left-handed twist that will cause you to look at a lot of commonly held concepts in a very different and useful manner. In the Appendix, I offer a summary of those left-handed rules and concepts. They have been well received by top executives of large corporations. Good as they are, you still need to train your managers.

Caring starts with perspective but requires more than compassion. It requires action. We need to view each other as unique and precious individuals and then treat one another with love and respect.

But as I said in the chapter on Women, you need to add an extension onto the Golden Rule; one which I trust the Rule's original author would permit me some license: Treat others the way you would want to be treated – <u>if you were them</u>!

Guys, don't treat women entirely like you would like to be treated. It's annoying. Boomers don't treat Millennials entirely like they're pursuing the American dream of the 60s and 70s. And Millennials, don't ignore the rules we've been living by our whole lives. Some of them actually work.

We've got to quit worrying about how other people act – including whole other generations - and start really concentrating on how we ourselves act. And when we act, we can't adhere to rules that arose from the Industrial Revolution that were designed to dehumanize people and turn them into instruments of production.[23] People are screaming for their individual humanity to be recognized.

If we start over in our thinking, we'll realize that all we've been doing is modifying those inhumane rules, playing catchup every generation with what people know is the right thing to do. Millennials are declaring those rules dead and we should applaud them for doing so and help them bury them in a managed transition to a new world that is 2 million years old. And we have to realize that the line between our job and the rest of our lives is blurring. So whatever we come up with has to fit our whole lives, not just our work lives.

So, I'll finish with a rule I posed to a group of managers at a company that was going through a big transition in their culture. I believe it is truly universal. But even if the rest of the universe won't adopt it, to the extent you adopt it, you and everyone else in your world will be better off.

Here's my final rule: We all play multiple roles in life: Father, mother, son, brother, daughter, sister, neighbor, coach, teacher, manager, employer, peer, coworker, ex-husband, citizen. The list goes on and changes from time to time. What

---

[23] Instruments of production? I sound like a Communist. I apologize, comrades. But the truth is, leftist movements always start with a foothold of some kind and then they pervert the cause and take over. The cure is always worse than the disease. So don't give them a foothold.

doesn't change is the need to play these roles unilaterally. In other words, be the best at what you do, regardless of how the other person in the relationship plays their role. Never make it contingent. Don't be the best brother only if your sister is the best sister. If you screwed up as a husband and the marriage fell apart, understand what she's going through now with the kids and be great in your new role as an ex. Don't be the best coach only if the athlete does everything he or she should. Take action and use discipline but don't withhold doing a great job. When that athlete, student, or employee leaves your charge someday, make sure they say you were the best coach, teacher, or manager they ever had.

This tincture of nobility is what has allowed us to survive as an amazingly social species for the last 2 million years. It might just get us through the next millennium.

APPENDIX

Summary of Concepts
A Lefthander's Guide to Management

Reprinted here from

A Guide to Managing Earthlings

by Charles Herrick

Summary of Concepts
A Lefthander's Guide to Management

To some people, left-handed thinking is simply untoward or not quite right. To others, especially those with a lefty in the family, you realize that we simply look at life just a little bit differently. Lefties can be handy to have around, especially if you are stuck on a problem that just won't seem to present a clear opening for resolution. Then sometimes, we lefties simply can't look at a problem the same way as everyone else, which makes it really handy to have right-handed people around.

Using a different lens and operating as a pre-med student who was always planning to leave the business world and go back to medicine, I built a way of looking at management that was useful to me. It made sense. It simplified things and then it let me use these simplified concepts to build new approaches to leading people and running a company. And then I wrote a book about it.

These are the concepts I present when I speak to groups of executives about management in general. They are also the concepts I adapt when I am asked to address hot topics such as the emergence of the Millennial culture and what to do about it. I suppose I look at this latter topic a bit differently as well. I think it's a great opportunity – if you don't drop the ball on the fundamentals of good management and decent behavior.

Most of these concepts were covered at various places in the book. Some are from other books I have written or they came from speaking engagements. Many of these are fairly unique, I am told. But some of them have been brought forth by others and I choose to put a different spin on them or merely reemphasize them because I think they have prematurely and inappropriately fallen into desuetude.

They're grouped logically to some extent and randomly here and there. That's the left-handed way.

A Manager Defined

1. Focus on What, not How. This has been the theme of this book [A Guide to Managing Earthlings].
2. Your job is to create problems for your people to solve. You are not the hero problem solver for your department. Identify the problems, set the objectives, measure the results, provide feedback and guidance. Repeat.
3. Management is a profession, not merely a role in a company.
4. Never forget the super-simplified role of a manager is to have the right people doing the right things. Get too far beyond that and you're a supervisor. That's a glorified word for a boss. Everyone wants a great manager and a true leader. Nobody wants a boss.
5. Deal in business issues, not personalities. You're a professional manager not a psychologist. You're a leader, not a manipulator.

6. A manager is a coach and counselor not a judge; a manager is a leader not a referee.
7. You are a manager because you have management skills. This is how it should be. It's not because you're smart or you sold the most widgets. EQ is way more important than IQ. I've got a lot of bruises from when I thought otherwise.
8. The most important desire a leader must have to be successful is to serve. Does that sound sanctimonious? Kind of a throwaway line that nobody dares argue with but you're all thinking, "That's a bunch of …stuff." But if a key business goal is to take care of the client and the employees are your front line for doing that, shouldn't you be doing everything to make sure they are able to do so? Figure out what they need to get their job done and then give it to them. That's service.

Vision and Purpose of your company

9. A great vision statement does not merely tell you what you are aiming to accomplish in the future; it changes who you are right now. I was just a kid but I remember Kennedy saying that by the end of the decade we were going to put a man on the moon. That got us out of the tit-for-tat race with the Soviet Union where they launched a satellite and then we launched a satellite; they sent a man into space and we sent a man into space. It changed who we were.

Instantly, we were no longer the "me too" guys, we were the guys who were going to the moon!
10. If you know who you are, you will know what to do. This is true for people as well as companies and organizations. Get an identity.
11. Average people believe you have to do a lot of things or do something big to be successful. Great people realize you have to be someone.
12. A true vision statement is complete and includes the mission and major milestones that when achieved will make the vision possible. If you present a vision statement without indicating you know and have a plan for the obvious big hurdles you will encounter, people won't buy in. Go read Kennedy's speech on going to the moon. He talks about all the things we would need to do to make it happen, including us believing we could do it.
13. Know what business you are really in. It's almost never in the name of your company. It tells you what your most important function is. When Xerox realized they were in the document management business and Harley realized they were in the nostalgia business, their fortunes turned around. Blue Cross is in the claims processing business. Starbucks is not in the coffee business. What business are you in?
14. Use the two hoops theory for every department. If you fire a missile at two imaginary hoops in the sky, separated by several miles, and it makes it through

both hoops, you are likely to hit your target. Know the two key measurements for each department and then don't bug 'em about the other ones unless they miss one of the hoops.

15. Avoid parallax – thinking you're all lined up on the same corporate objective when you really aren't. If managers only a couple of levels down from the CEO makes their targets, the CEO should make his. But the CEO has to know for sure. Know your top two objectives and then find out what the top two objectives of your direct reports are plus the top two objectives of his direct reports are. It takes 10 minutes. By the way, your direct reports should know two levels down as well.

16. I never wanted to know more than the one or two key things any of my direct reports were pursuing. Anything beyond that I could call his or her secretary and ask. Work on big stuff. And make sure your direct reports are working on big stuff.

Manager as a coach and counselor

17. You must earn the right to criticize, even if you're the boss. To truly criticize you must already be established as a trusted collaborator, well in advance. This is critical when dealing with Millennials.

18. Performance must become a third party object that you and the employee can put on the table and discuss. Do this even if the employee is way behind: "Fred, you were supposed to be at point X but

you're only at point Y, what's needed to close the gap? What can I do to help?"

19. If you have made it clear to the employee that you are there to help them in their career and working only in their best interest, then and only then, can you treat performance like a third party object.

20. Never ask adults to justify themselves or their behavior. Avoid the use of the word "Why?" When you ask, "What happened?" it makes people a lot less defensive than when you say, "Why did you do that?" By the way, the age at which this gives better results starts at 4 years old. Try it.

21. Certain management types will never be in position to offer ongoing coaching and counseling. If your style requires that people defend themselves even occasionally, they will do that first and then maybe they'll talk about business objectively – but probably not. Survival trumps business.

22. Powder puff appraisals, focusing only on the positive, are a copout and an extension of the self-esteem movement. It's essentially an admission of failure to establish trust.

23. When critiquing or giving feedback, talk about general reaction and overall positives first. Talk about the big stuff and then the little stuff. Discuss negatives only if you have to and then secondarily. Consider mentioning trivial stuff in a separate, oh-by-the-way conversation to avoid looking trivial or making the employee feel like something trivial just

took away from his or her good work. Think about how you feel when you are criticized. I personally hate it. This is mostly due to a lifetime of being counseled by insensitive jerks, who have taken advantage of their position to treat a subordinate in a way they would never treat someone whose relationship they truly valued.

Decision Making

24. Decisions are made by verifying a gut feel, not by weighing the pros and cons. You're an executive, not an accountant. You will always have less information than you need for big decisions.
25. Make the decision and then clean up the mess.
26. Big decisions almost always hurt someone. Big decisions that are delayed hurt almost everyone.
27. Seeking consensus is for weaklings. Allow for constant input. Collaborate to the extent necessary and then make the decision.

Humane Management and Tribal Instincts

28. Humane management has two components: Caring and Competence. Caring alone won't do it. Working for a manager who is lousy at the many functions of management is miserable. It hurts people who count on you. It's inhumane.
29. Caring is an act not a feeling. Compassion is a feeling. True caring is putting compassion into action.

30. We are tribal creatures with an innate desire to belong permanently. Make people feel secure, even if it costs you in a specific instance.
31. The industrial revolution was the first time we made an institution out of non-tribal behaviors in that for the first time people could routinely be kicked out of the tribe at will. By continuing this practice, we are creating an environment that defies 2 million years of human development.
32. Note to CEOs: You are the head of your tribe. Your number one constituency is your people, not your customers, not your shareholders. Never forget that. And never let your people forget that you won't forget that. CEOs who say the customer is number one are abrading delicate human instincts and making it clear that their people are just cogs in an organic machine. Making sure your customers and shareholders think they are at the top of your list falls under the CEO function called diplomacy.

Morale and the three Utility functions of management

33. You can manage morale via two levers: Creating a sense that the company is going to do well and regularly performing the utility functions of management:
    a. Communication
    b. Delegation
    c. Recognition of performance

34. People must feel heard. It's not good enough that you hear them. They must feel it. If they don't they'll find someone else who will make them feel heard. That other person may not be acting in your best interest or the company's best interest. That's the practical reason. The humane reason is that it hurts not to be heard. People today often feel very lonely at work. Fix that.
35. Good and timely communication makes people feel valued, not just informed.
36. Employee opinion surveys are too often viewed by the employee as their one shot at letting you know how messed up things are. It should not be that way. The opinion survey is a process that should have employee involvement even in the design. Employees need to know it will be an iterative process with multiple avenues for feedback. If companies fail to do this, they will simply be setting themselves up for the biggest salvos the employees can launch to make sure they get heard and maybe even responded to.
37. Delegation makes people feel good about themselves. It gives them worth. Done right, it allows people to achieve *your* objectives *their* way, which is always more efficient and effective. It allows them to think about it long enough to perhaps come back and tell you that they ought not to do it at all. Only great managers have this kind of relationship with their direct reports.

38. Some people can't delegate even if they want to. If you are a perfectionist or in any way punitive, people won't do it their way, they will spend all their time trying to figure out how you would like them to do it. Start cutting your people some slack for your own good. That may sound selfish but if you're perfectionist or punitive, you're already a selfish person. I'm just giving you some tips and appealing to the only avenue open to persuade you.
39. Recognition is done in a variety of ways, every day. If people aren't recognized for their work, they feel devalued. Who wants a bunch of people working for them who feel lousy about themselves? I'll tell you, egotists who have a need to be the most important and valuable person. If you can't get there on merit, then devalue others. Productivity suffers but egotists feel bigger somehow.
40. People who constantly make people feel like they should have done a little better are true jerks. Some people think this is a clever way to get people to close the performance gap. It's not. It makes people give up and then adopt a variety of masking behaviors to get by. Millennials won't even fake it. They're too honest. They'll just shut down.
41. Most managers can't list three reasons why their employees come to work every day. That's sad. What's even sadder is that most employees can't either. Give them lots of reasons.

Management Power

42. Great managers increase their power by extending maximum power to the people that report to them. It almost defies the laws of physics. I'm as fascinated by this as I am by hydraulics and compound interest. It's magic. Try it.
43. Power comes from two sources: Respect or some form of coercion. Leaders are respected and can draw on the power in people to get things done. Bosses must use energy to get people moving and keep them moving.
44. If you aren't any good at the job of managing, people will eventually have little respect for you and you will have to resort to coercion in its many forms. Managers need training.
45. Moody managers divert people's energy. Your employees go from solving business problems to appeasing your moods and timing their actions or requests for your "good" days. How is that good for business?
46. Another form of coercion is trying to be popular. As a manager, never run for Homecoming Queen. You'll lose, even if you're the only one running. You can't lead based on popularity and people liking you. It's a pitiful form of coercion.

Turnover

47. Turnover is a consequence of disconnectedness. You must have a strategy that makes people feel both secure and connected. Some people call this

disenfranchisement. I would use that word if I thought anyone I asked could possibly define the word "enfranchisement."

48. Turnover prevention begins at hiring. Employee orientation as a goal in itself is inadequate. The goal must be assimilation and there must be a formal program, involving multiple levels of managers over an extended period of time.

49. People quit most often because of a fear of their own imminent failure in their performance or in their relationships. Institute programs that make it nearly impossible to fire employees and people will no longer quit. Instead, they will divert their energies from defense to offense and start trying to get ahead.

50. Never let a person feel they have permanently fallen from grace.

51. Firing someone is a violent act. You harm or destroy families, career plans, college plans, retirement plans. You are firing a spouse and kids too.

52. When you fire someone it has a systemic effect. It disrupts people's sense of security throughout the company. Firing someone who deserves it is not okay either. One thing people should never pray for is justice. I thank God, literally, that I haven't always gotten what I deserve. You should too. Now pay that forward and show the lack of justice you've benefited from for decades.

53. Not firing someone who deserves it demonstrates grace and mercy and improves people's sense of security. In a company of 100 or more employees, you can almost always find another role for the person. You have many levers to pull besides firing: reassignment, demotion, pay cuts until they are back on track, etc. Be creative. There's a real human being and his or her family involved.

Solving the supposed Millennial "Crisis"

54. View it as an incredible opportunity. If you can't do that, please tell me how you're going to skip an entire generation. There are 82 million of them. I work with them all the time. They are sharp. Sometimes they seem rude but they're so honest and coachable, you can just point out stuff that bugs you – unless of course you have zero relationship with them. If that's the case, get used to people texting while you're telling them about your mother's last words on her deathbed.
55. Millennials are incredibly underutilized. Millennials got well educated, were told they could be anything they set their mind on becoming, and then when they hatched in about 2006, the world fell apart. They got screwed. They are chronically depressed. Start treating them well and see what happens. Start giving them real assignments and big jobs. You'll be amazed. They're just like us.

56. Follow the three "secret" investment strategies I learned while I was at IBM:
    a. Invest during downturns while everyone else is hiding under their desk.
    b. Invest in management. It's an asset layer, not overhead. Get some ROI out of it. People quit investing in management training about a decade ago and look where we are now with awful morale and high turnover.
    c. Only hire A players. They are worth three times as much as B players but they don't cost three times as much.
57. Do three counter-intuitive things with Millennials
    a. Depersonalize the management process to improve your personal relationship with all employees. That's what this whole book has been about. If you can't get performance to the level of an object discussed by two colleagues, you are not going to cut it with Millennials or anyone else. They'll quit and move back home. Over one third of them have done it.
    b. You must commit to the relationship first. Giving them a job is not a personal commitment. Did you use up a hiring ticket? Big deal. They just changed their life to come work for you. The days of giving up one's whole life for the company are over. So get out in front of it.

c. To the extent possible, adjust to their lifestyle. It's not that hard. It's the way work has been done for all but about two hundred of the last two million years. I'm a laissez faire capitalist but I honestly can't distinguish much between old style industrialism and slavery. The world is going to change. The question we have as managers and executives is this: are we going to lead that change or are we going to have it happen to us?

Two things I frequently say to clients who are in difficulty:

58. You don't have 17 problems, you have one or two. Let's figure them out and the other 15 or 16 will recede in importance or, better said, urgency.
59. You are not going to fine-tune your way out of this mess. You need to take bold action and you have to be right. Just because you're surrounded, doesn't mean you can attack in any direction. Let's find the right place to focus your energy and then apply everything you've got.

Universal rule for what to do.

We all play multiple roles in life: Father, mother, son, brother, daughter, sister, neighbor, coach, teacher, manager, employer, peer, coworker, ex-husband, citizen. The list goes on and changes from time to time. What doesn't change is the need to play these roles unilaterally. In other words, be the best at what you do, regardless of how the other person in the relationship plays their role. Never make it contingent. Don't be the best brother only if your sister is the best sister. If you screwed up as a husband and the marriage fell apart, understand what she's going through now with the kids and be a great ex. Don't be the best coach only if the athlete does everything he or she should. Take action and use discipline but don't withhold doing a great job. When that athlete, student, or employee leaves your charge someday, make sure they say you were the best coach, teacher, or manager they ever had.

About the Author

Charles is a Seattle native and a longtime resident of planet Earth. He married Kristy while in college and he feels that was the best decision of his life. They have three great kids, Lexie, Mason and Walker, along with llamas, two chickens and a bulldog named Bullard, who is very dull and dependent.

With a Bachelor of Science degree in pre-medical studies and fresh out of the University of Washington, Charles took the next logical step. He started his career at IBM in the group that sold the behemoth mainframes, despite the fact that he was the only one of 228 applicants that had never seen a computer.

He diligently stuck with his preparations to go to medical school for over 17 years, moving in and out of IBM field and headquarters jobs. Finally, it was time. He left his position as the head of the IBM consulting group in the Northwest and took over as CEO for a high-end micro-roaster in the burgeoning Seattle coffee market.

With a solid understanding of both regular and decaf, he then stepped in and ran a large software integration firm, building it from 700 (mostly miserable) employees to where it was the dominant IT consulting firm in the Northwest, with over 1500 (mostly happy) employees. Next, he and his colleague Bill Douglass started and sold their own IT consulting firm.

Of the 5000 people in Seattle who have worked for Charles at one time or another, approximately 80% love him; 15% could take him or leave him; and 5% will run him over in a crosswalk if they see him. This is an admirable distribution and one we should all strive for – especially if you look both ways when crossing the street.

He took a multi-year sabbatical and went alone to the mud huts of Kenya, the slums of Bombay, Afghanistan and other places rarely mentioned in Condé Nast. There he resolved an epidemic, treated lepers and untouchables for all kinds of health ailments, and taught a woman in a remote village to walk again who had been crippled for 33 years. He is now reluctantly back in the business world where he would prefer to consult rather than work.

Charles also competes internationally in Masters Track and Field in the 400 meter dash. In 2012 he was the Silver Medalist in the 400 meters at the USA Track and Field Masters National Championships in Chicago.

Charles is the author of *A Guide to Managing Earthlings*, an enlightening, left-handed application of his IBM management training to the new world of business. He also wrote *Breath of Kenya*, which tells a gripping story of his time in a primitive village in the deep interior of East Africa.

Check out his other works listed at the beginning of this book.

Email the author: charles@charlesherrick.com

www.ingramcontent.com/pod-product-compliance
Lightning Source LLC
Chambersburg PA
CBHW020915180526
45163CB00007B/2739